The Black Briefcase

The Black Briefcase

Matthew Petchinsky

1

The Black Briefcase: How MiB Stay Wealthy in Silence

By: Matthew Petchinsky

Disclaimer

This book, *The Black Briefcase: How MiB Stay Wealthy in Silence*, is an entirely **unofficial** and **independently created financial guide**. It draws creative and metaphorical inspiration from the themes, aesthetic, and storytelling elements associated with the *Men in Black* film universe for the sole purpose of **entertaining and educating** readers on financial principles in a unique and memorable way. This book **does not represent, reflect, or claim any affiliation with, sponsorship by, or endorsement from Sony Pictures Entertainment Inc., Columbia Pictures, Amblin Entertainment, or any rights holders of the *Men in Black* franchise.**

All characters, organizations, terminology, gadgets, or imagery referenced or reimagined within this guide are used **purely for thematic illustration** and **satirical commentary**, intended to add narrative flair to real-world strategies for personal finance, wealth building, income protection, and long-term asset growth. No copyrighted materials, scripts, or licensed intellectual property from the *Men in Black* films are used or replicated.

This book does not claim to train agents, unlock top-secret vaults, or grant access to alien economies. It is a **financial literacy tool** wrapped in an imaginative metaphor, designed to help readers apply covert-level focus, discipline, and discretion to their financial lives—no neuralyzer required.

Any names, situations, or similarities to real persons or government entities are purely coincidental or fictionalized. This is a creative work protected under fair use guidelines for parody, satire, and educational commentary.

Readers are advised to consult a licensed financial advisor, accountant, or attorney before making major financial decisions. This guide provides general information only and does not constitute professional or personalized financial advice.

In short: **This is not an official Men in Black product. This is your unofficial financial field manual.** Let the agents of your wealth operate in silence—and let your results make the noise.

Introduction

The Black Briefcase: How MiB Stay Wealthy in Silence

True wealth doesn't wear designer labels. It doesn't flash watches, flaunt cars, or fight for attention. It whispers. It waits. It moves through systems without setting off alarms. In a world where social media tells you that success is about going viral, this book invites you to go invisible.

Inspired by the shadowy professionalism and calm control of the Men in Black, this guide redefines what it means to be wealthy. Not with galactic gadgets or alien technologies—but with real-world strategies rooted in discretion, discipline, and deep strategy. If you've ever wondered how some people always seem ahead of the curve yet are never in the spotlight, this book reveals the mindset and mechanics behind their silent success.

The Black Briefcase isn't about stashing cash in offshore accounts or learning Wall Street wizardry. It's about building a financial empire beneath the radar. It's about quiet power—the kind that doesn't need recognition to be real. Like the agents who erase memories and walk away unnoticed, true financial mastery leaves no trace but changes everything.

Here, you'll learn the fundamentals of **financial stealth**:

- How to build wealth without drawing attention
- How to manage your money like an agent, not a gambler
- How to vanish from financial traps and reappear in new positions of power
- How to protect what you've built from exposure, envy, and exploitation

This is not your typical get-rich book. There are no loud promises, no golden secrets, and no get-rich-quick schemes. What you will find is a toolkit for *long-term wealth without chaos*. A manual for thriving in silence. A blueprint for becoming the kind of person who doesn't need to be seen to be successful.

The goal? Not to be rich and known.

The goal? To be **secure, sovereign, and silent.**

So suit up. Open the black briefcase. Inside are the principles of hidden wealth that most will never see—and that's exactly the point.

Chapter 1: Your Life Is Classified

Why Privacy Is the First Rule of Money Mastery

In the world of the Men in Black, agents don't exist on paper. Their lives are classified. Their identities are erased. Their movements are never tracked. To the public, they're invisible. And yet—they hold the keys to planetary secrets, intergalactic diplomacy, and technology beyond human comprehension. Their greatest asset isn't just their training. It's their anonymity.

And so it is with true wealth.

When it comes to building financial power, **privacy isn't optional—it's foundational**. Before a single dollar is invested, before a business is started, before an account is opened, the first step is this: **protect your personal data, decisions, and direction.** Because in today's world, visibility is vulnerability.

The Wealth Trap of Oversharing

Social media platforms have conditioned millions to believe that success must be seen to be real. We document achievements, purchases, vacations, and even financial milestones in public view. But this digital exhibitionism comes at a high cost:

- **Predators know where to strike.** Whether it's identity thieves, jealous peers, or opportunistic relatives, the more visible your gains, the more you attract unnecessary attention.
- **Governments and corporations track spending behavior.** Every post, every financial move, becomes metadata that can be sold, taxed, or targeted.
- **Your strategy becomes exposed.** When people know what you're doing, they can block, copy, or sabotage it.

You can't build a secure empire with a spotlight on every brick.

The Agent Mindset: Silent Moves, Loud Results

Men in Black agents operate under the highest levels of classification for one reason: **impact without interference**. They don't need the world to know they saved it. They need the world *not to notice*. You must adopt the same mindset.

Here's how to think like a classified agent of wealth:

- **Keep your goals offline.** Not everyone deserves to know what you're working on. Let results speak louder than announcements.
- **Operate from need-to-know.** Only share your plans with those who directly contribute to them—or not at all.
- **Silence is your security system.** When people don't know what you have, they can't take it, sabotage it, or tax it prematurely.

Practical Financial Privacy Protocols

You don't need sunglasses and a neuralyzer to protect your financial data—you just need systems that minimize exposure and maximize discretion:

1. Use Privacy-Focused Financial Tools

- Open accounts with institutions that allow for two-factor authentication and end-to-end encryption.
- Consider financial tools that prioritize anonymity (like privacy-focused budgeting apps or virtual bank cards).

2. Build Business Structures, Not Just Accounts

- Form an LLC or trust for asset protection. It separates your identity from your income.
- Use EINs (Employer Identification Numbers) instead of your Social Security Number when possible.

3. Avoid Financial Oversharing

- Never disclose your income streams, investments, or net worth on public platforms.
- Be cautious even in private conversations. People have long memories and short ethics.

4. Create Separate Digital Identities

- Use different email addresses, phone numbers, and profiles for personal, business, and investment activities.
- Consider a VPN when accessing sensitive accounts or researching investment strategies.

The Danger of Letting Others In Too Soon

Letting the wrong people into your financial world is like showing an alien your tech—just because you can doesn't mean you should. From partnerships that sour to relatives who leech, history is full of stories where oversharing cost empires.

Trust must be **earned through results**, not assumed through relationships.

Your finances are not a group project.
Your vision doesn't need validation.
Your wealth doesn't need applause.

The Silence Test: Can You Keep It Quiet?

Ask yourself:

- Can you hit a major financial milestone without telling anyone?
- Can you resist the urge to "flex" on social media when you win?
- Can you stay humble when you've earned what others only dream of?

If the answer is yes, you're ready to operate like an agent.
If not, you're still too loud to lead.

Conclusion: Hidden Power Is the Safest Power

There's a reason classified documents are locked away. Their value demands protection. Your life, your goals, your wealth-building journey should be treated the same way.

Because the minute you go public with your plans, you invite scrutiny, sabotage, and spiritual interference. But when you move in silence, there are no weak points. No leaks. No breaches. Only steady, undetectable progress.

So from this moment forward, remember:
Your life is classified.

Your mission is silent.
And your wealth is nobody's business but yours.

The briefcase is closed. The suit is on.

Let's begin.

Chapter 2: Black Suit Budgeting

Spend Like an Agent: Sharp, Controlled, Deadly Efficient

The black suit is more than just a uniform. It's a symbol of precision, professionalism, and control. Men in Black agents don't wear it for fashion. They wear it because it communicates one message: *I'm here on mission*. Every crease, every accessory, every movement serves a purpose.

That's exactly how your budget should operate—**disciplined, strategic, and mission-oriented**. No flash. No waste. No unnecessary movements. In this chapter, we're suiting up your spending habits for covert operations in the world of personal finance.

What Is Black Suit Budgeting?

Black Suit Budgeting is a financial approach modeled after the quiet intensity of field agents. It's not minimalist for the sake of deprivation, nor is it frugal to the point of self-denial. Instead, it's **streamlined wealth discipline**—spending that reflects high-level control with zero tolerance for leakage, bloat, or emotional detours.

It answers one question with every transaction:

"Does this serve the mission?"

If the answer is no, the wallet stays closed.

The Mission Budget vs. Civilian Budget

Civilian budgeting focuses on surviving and stretching. It's reactive. It trims down only when pressure hits.

Agent-level budgeting, by contrast, is proactive. It's based on long-term operations. Think like this:

Civilian Mentality	Black Suit Mentality
"Can I afford this?"	"Does this serve the mission?"
Buys on emotion	Buys on strategy
Seeks comfort	Prioritizes growth
Tracks spending monthly	Tracks *momentum* weekly
Cuts costs under stress	Optimizes always

The Four Commandments of Black Suit Budgeting

1. Identify Your Core Directives (Spending Categories)

Every agent has a mission profile. Yours begins with identifying the **non-negotiables**—the operational costs that directly support your wealth-building journey.

Break your life into three primary categories:

- **Mission-Critical Expenses** – Rent, transportation, work tools, basic food and health.
- **Stealth Growth Expenses** – Education, investing, skill-building, business scaling.
- **Containment Costs** – Entertainment, social events, non-essential purchases.

The secret? Prioritize the first two. **Mission-critical and stealth growth keep you moving forward. Containment costs keep you stuck.**

2. Automate Everything You Can

An agent doesn't wake up wondering what to do. Their routine is automated. You should do the same with your money.

- Set up **automatic transfers** into your savings and investment accounts the moment your income arrives.
- Use **auto-pay** on mission-critical bills to prevent late fees and unnecessary attention from creditors.
- Eliminate decision fatigue by removing daily financial choices from your plate. *More automation = fewer mistakes.*

3. Run Budget Drills Weekly

Agents debrief constantly. Your finances need the same attention. Conduct a **weekly financial review** every Sunday (or your preferred planning day).

- Scan every expense. Ask: *"Was this stealthy or sloppy?"*
- Adjust upcoming week's discretionary spending to reflect new intelligence.
- Update your net worth, account balances, or key milestones.

You're not budgeting to survive—you're reviewing to improve **operational precision.**

4. Kill Lifestyle Creep with Ruthless Logic

Agents don't get sloppy in the field. You can't get sloppy with spending.

Just because you earn more doesn't mean you should spend more. That's **lifestyle creep**, and it's the civilian equivalent of blowing your cover.

Instead of rewarding yourself with "stuff," reward yourself with:

- Buying **time freedom** (outsourcing tasks)
- Funding **new business ops**
- Investing in **long-term sovereignty**

If it doesn't buy back time, grow your income, or expand your power—it's not worth it.

Gear Up: Tools for Covert Budgeting

Treat your financial tools like agent gadgets—choose only those that enhance performance:

- **Encrypted budgeting apps** like Monarch, YNAB, or Cube for stealth planning
- **Prepaid debit cards** for discretionary spending caps
- **Separate accounts**: one for fixed ops (bills), one for flexible missions (discretionary), and one vault (investments/savings)
- **Code names** in your banking memos. Instead of "Netflix," call it "Operation Relaxation." Keeps you in mission mode.

The Agent's Emergency Fund: Your Escape Vehicle

Every agent has a way out when things go south. You need a **financial extraction plan**—your emergency fund.

Target:

- **$1,000** for short-term sabotage
- **3–6 months of living expenses** for full operations suspension

This is your *untraceable lifeline*. No emotional purchases. No leaks. It exists to protect your freedom, not fund your fears.

Black Briefcase Bonus: Stealth Spending Techniques

- **Decoy Fund**: Keep a low visible balance in checking while the real funds sit elsewhere.
- **Ghost Subscriptions Audit**: Monthly, track every recurring charge and cancel any non-mission expense.
- **Invisible Income Method**: Each time you get paid, act like 30% never existed—hide it in a separate account and never look back.

Conclusion: Be the Budget, Not the Bling

Black Suit Budgeting isn't about looking wealthy. It's about **becoming untouchably, quietly powerful**.

It's about cultivating a relationship with money that doesn't depend on how much you spend—but how efficiently you operate.

So from now on:

- No emotional buys.
- No loose ends.
- No chaos.

Just clean lines, clean moves, clean ledgers.

Every dollar is a directive.
Every choice is tactical.
Every expense is either a mission... or a mistake.

Suit up. Budget sharp. And leave no financial footprint behind.

Chapter 3: Income from the Shadows

Build Side Income No One Expects

In the *Men in Black* universe, agents don't clock into ordinary jobs. Their salaries don't come from public pay stubs or LinkedIn résumés. They operate off-grid, under-the-radar, and far beyond what anyone would suspect. Yet despite their anonymity, they're well-funded, well-equipped, and always ready.

This is your new income model.

True wealth isn't just earned—it's engineered quietly. In this chapter, we go deep into how to build multiple income streams that flow silently, consistently, and without fanfare. This isn't about becoming an influencer or chasing viral attention. It's about creating sustainable, off-the-books-style earnings that **secure your freedom** without broadcasting your ascent.

Welcome to the art of earning in the shadows.

The Core Principle: Visibility = Vulnerability

When your income is loud and public:

- It invites questions.
- It attracts dependents.
- It becomes taxable and traceable.

But when your income is diversified and low-profile:

- It's harder to sabotage.
- It gives you leverage others can't measure.
- It builds real resilience, not performance-based income.

Income from the shadows means **quiet profit with zero dependency on applause**.

The 5 Traits of Shadow-Grade Income Streams

To qualify as "shadow income," a stream must meet most of these criteria:

1. **Low visibility** – Not linked to your full name or daily identity.
2. **Scalable without exposure** – Grows with automation or systems, not personal branding.
3. **Tax-prepped but discrete** – Can be reported legally if desired, but doesn't scream "entrepreneur."
4. **Emotionally detached** – Not reliant on ego, followers, or public feedback.
5. **Mobile and flexible** – Operates from anywhere, at any time, without needing your face on it.

Now let's build yours.

Covert Income Stream #1: Anonymous Digital Products

Digital goods are the agent's weapon of choice—no inventory, no physical presence, and unlimited duplication.

Examples:

- **Ebooks or guides** under a pen name
- **Printable planners or workbooks** sold on Etsy or Gumroad
- **Course PDFs** on niche skills like language learning, coding basics, or magick systems
- **Stock music, templates, or mockups** for creators

Stealth Tip: Use a business alias and non-identifiable branding. Funnel all income through a business PayPal or LLC-linked Stripe account. Silence is built into the system.

Covert Income Stream #2: Print-on-Demand & Merchandise

You don't need a clothing line—you need a **silent wardrobe funnel**.

Use services like:

- Redbubble
- TeePublic
- Spreadshirt
- Printify + Etsy

Create:

- Minimalist quotes
- Parody designs
- AI-generated art with your unique themes
- Obscure niche merch (for fandoms, local towns, or holidays)

Design once, and get paid in the background. Even better? You'll earn while staying invisible.

Covert Income Stream #3: Digital Services with Code Names

Offer services—but not under your main name. Use pseudonyms or project names.

Options:

- **Ghostwriting** for other entrepreneurs
- **Virtual assistance** (email management, customer service, transcription)
- **Podcast editing**
- **Book formatting**
- **Research or proofreading**

Platforms like Fiverr, Upwork, and Contra allow you to set up profiles that don't include your personal identity.

Operate under the radar. Provide elite service. Build quiet clientele.

Covert Income Stream #4: Passive Royalties from Micro Assets

Royalties = agent-level cash flow. You create once, then disappear while the system pays you.

Sources:

- **KDP self-published books** (fiction or nonfiction under various pen names)
- **Audiobooks** using text-to-speech or AI narration tools
- **Music loops or beats** for video creators
- **Low-content journals** and notebooks

Every shadow operation needs **a trail of income-producing ghosts.**

Covert Income Stream #5: Affiliate Networks & Referral Cash

An agent doesn't always create—they redirect.

With affiliate income, you recommend someone else's tool or product. When someone buys, you get paid. No customer service. No inventory.

Niches that work:

- Finance (credit card tools, budgeting apps)
- Wellness (supplements, fitness plans)
- Tech (VPNs, browser tools, AI apps)
- Education (language platforms, online courses)

Stealth Tip: Use **redirect links** and track traffic without ever revealing your real identity. Operate as a faceless recommender. Just the shadows—and clicks.

Covert Income Stream #6: Marketplace Arbitrage

The field agents of finance often profit in ways others overlook. One classic method? **Buy low, sell higher. Silently.**

Examples:

- **Book arbitrage:** Buy discounted used books, resell on Amazon FBA.
- **Vintage flipping:** Source items from thrift stores and flip on eBay or Poshmark.
- **Niche resale:** Collect toys, electronics, or rare goods for hidden profits.

No one needs to know you're flipping oddities. The cash flows. You disappear. Just like an agent would.

How to Operate Multiple Streams Silently

To manage a silent income system:

1. **Assign code names** to each stream (e.g., "Project Nebula" = your KDP books; "Echo-4" = your ghostwriting profile).
2. **Route earnings to one centralized command account** (ideally a business account).
3. **Use private tracking sheets** to monitor growth.
4. **Avoid cross-posting** across personal platforms. Keep everything compartmentalized.

The Extraction Rule: Cash Flow Over Clout

Here's what civilians don't get:

Real power isn't how loud you earn—it's how long you last.

Earning $1,000 a month from three stealth streams is worth more than $10,000 that depends on being famous, active, or constantly online.

Your goal: **durable, distributed, disappearing income.** No single point of failure. No ego attached. Just money that moves without you.

Conclusion: Leave No Trace, Earn Every Dollar

When you build income in the shadows:

- No one questions where it came from.
- No one sees it coming.
- No one can take it from you.

That's the beauty of financial silence. You don't just protect your future—you make it immune to interference.

So while others scream for attention...

You'll be building a kingdom under cover.

Just you. A black briefcase.

And a mission funded from the shadows.

Chapter 4: Emergency Exit Wealth

Create Financial Exit Plans for Every Scenario

Every Men in Black agent knows: **no mission is guaranteed to go according to plan.** That's why there's always a way out—an escape pod, a neuralyzer, a wormhole, or a black sedan with untraceable plates waiting in the alley. Survival isn't luck. It's preparation. It's calculated contingency. It's having an exit route before the danger appears.

And when it comes to wealth, the same principle applies.

In a world of inflation spikes, job loss, housing collapses, family betrayals, sudden medical bills, and government overreach, you must be ready to **disappear financially and reappear with power.** This chapter equips you with "Emergency Exit Wealth"—your personalized, protected escape plan for *any* scenario.

Whether the threat is economic, emotional, environmental, or systemic—you'll have a way out.

What Is Emergency Exit Wealth?

Emergency Exit Wealth isn't about having a savings account. It's about building a multi-layered *financial survival system*—a structure designed to allow you to:

- Leave your job at a moment's notice
- Escape a toxic household or relationship
- Pivot from a failing business
- Survive six months without income
- Relocate across the country—or the planet—without starting over

It's not "Plan B."

It's **Plan Get-Out-Now.**

And it needs to be activated before the threat arrives.

The 4 Levels of Financial Escape Planning

To build true Emergency Exit Wealth, you need layered strategies. Each level assumes a deeper level of threat.

Level 1: Buffer and Bounce

Threat: Temporary job loss, sudden bill, minor crisis
Response: Access liquid cash and exit short-term obligations

- **Goal**: $1,000–$3,000 stored in ultra-liquid form (accessible within 24 hours)
- **Tools**:
    - High-yield savings account
    - Prepaid debit card with stored funds
    - Cash envelope (for disasters or tech outages)

Agent Tip: Store at least $200 in physical cash in a waterproof, fire-proof container at home—label it *"Extraction Only."*

Level 2: Disengage and Relocate

Threat: Toxic job, abusive household, unexpected eviction, economic downturn
Response: Fund relocation, replace lost income, and reset quietly

- **Goal**: 3–6 months of living expenses in a separate, secure account
- **Tools**:
    - Online-only bank accounts not tied to your main bank
    - Pre-booked Airbnbs or cheap relocation options bookmarked in a hidden folder
    - Stored digital income (ebooks, print-on-demand, affiliate) generating passive flow

Agent Tip: Create a fake "vacation savings" account to hide these funds emotionally from yourself and others. It's not a trip. It's your exit ticket.

Level 3: Identity and Infrastructure Reboot

Threat: Legal issues, identity theft, public fallout, systemic collapse
Response: Shift income sources, reroute identity, and rebuild operational base

- **Goal**: Financial sovereignty without needing old credentials
- **Tools**:
  - LLC or business structure with separate EIN and tax identity
  - Anonymous domains and pseudonyms for digital income
  - Cloud-based backups of every asset: IDs, credentials, passwords, key documents
  - VPN and encrypted browser extensions for safe access

Agent Tip: Create a **digital bug-out drive**—a password-protected USB with everything you'd need to restart remotely. Include financial ledgers, resumes, contracts, and business logins.

Level 4: Total Extraction and Sovereign Life

Threat: Civil unrest, massive system failure, martial law, targeted persecution

Response: Self-sustain abroad or in rural seclusion, with complete autonomy

- **Goal**: Rebuild life in a new place without dependence on your old ecosystem
- **Tools**:
    - Citizenship or residency plan in another country (second passport, D7 visa, etc.)
    - Land fund or property acquisition account (for remote retreat, off-grid survival, etc.)
    - Precious metals or decentralized crypto (held offline)
    - Skills-based income source (survival skills, bartering, teaching, digital freelancing)

Agent Tip: Keep a hidden document called *"Operation Nowhere"* outlining how, when, and where you would relocate if needed—include financial contacts, land options, and a stripped-down cost-of-living analysis.

Emergency Exit Fund Rules (Agent Grade)

1. **Never name it 'Emergency Fund' in your bank**
   Call it something meaningless to others—*"Station Z"*, *"Blue Archive"*, or *"Project Vega."*
2. **Don't store all funds in one institution**
   If your bank is frozen or fails, you need alternatives.
3. **Use financial decoys**
   Let people see a "main" checking account with predictable movements. Keep real wealth behind a different firewall.
4. **Don't delay activation**
   The worst time to prepare is after the problem has begun. Every mission has a countdown. Start building now.

Emergency Income Activation Protocol

Even if you escape the threat, you'll still need cashflow. Prepare side hustles or scalable systems you can activate immediately:

- **Freelance skills you can offer with a pseudonym**
- **Backlist of books, printables, or courses to reupload under a new identity**
- **Crypto wallet addresses ready for international donations or anonymous business**

This is your post-extraction firepower. Income without exposure.

Emotional Wealth Extraction

Emergency Exit Wealth isn't just physical—it's psychological.

- Create a **"No-Contact Budget"**: What would it cost to emotionally detach from everyone who drains you?
- Fund your **Quiet Exit Therapy Fund**: Sometimes, leaving isn't about fleeing danger—it's about healing in peace.
- Build your **No-Strings Attached Fund**: Enough money to say "No" without guilt, "I'm done" without debate, and "I choose peace" without hesitation.

That's freedom wealth.

The kind that's not just smart. It's *sovereign.*

Conclusion: Always Have a Way Out

An agent never enters a building without knowing how to exit it. Neither should you enter a job, a lease, a relationship, or a city without knowing how to walk away—*with your wealth intact.*

Emergency Exit Wealth isn't fear-based.

It's **freedom-based**.

It's knowing you don't have to stay anywhere that betrays your peace.

Your black briefcase isn't just full of money.

It's full of escape codes.

And if the world goes dark...

You already have the map.

Chapter 5: The Neuralyzer Method

How to Disappear Debt and Reprogram Abundance

In the *Men in Black* universe, the Neuralyzer is a sleek, silver device with one extraordinary function: **it erases memory**. A single flash, and the past vanishes—clean, painless, and immediate. Victims forget alien encounters, conspiracies, and catastrophes like they never happened.

You might wish you could use one on your bank account.

The truth is, many people walk through life mentally chained to their financial past. Old mistakes. Bad credit. Crushing debt. Years of guilt, shame, and scarcity. These patterns don't just linger—they *program* your future.

But what if you could Neuralyze your money story?

What if you could erase financial trauma—not by forgetting it, but by *reprogramming your response to it*?

Welcome to the Neuralyzer Method: a mind-reset protocol for eliminating the emotional grip of debt, replacing it with stealth wealth strategies and a deep internal shift toward **abundance that lasts.**

Your Debt Is a Memory, Not a Destiny

Debt is not a life sentence. It's a data point. A number. A symptom of a system designed to exploit emotional spending, misinformation, and a lack of early education.

But here's the secret agents know:

The past is editable. The future is programmable.

To erase debt's power over you, you must start with the narrative, not the numbers.

Phase 1: Identify the Invasive Memory

Before a Neuralyzer flash, agents identify the memory that must be deleted. You'll do the same.

Ask yourself:

- What moment in your financial past haunts you the most?
- What is the single money belief you've been repeating for years?
- Who convinced you that wealth wasn't for people like you?

Write it down. Get it out. Expose the memory. Because what stays in the dark controls you.

Now prepare to flash it.

Phase 2: Flash the Neuralyzer – Emotional Reset Protocol
To truly reset, we must interrupt the emotional loop. Here's how:
The Flash Technique (Mental Neuralyzer Ritual):

1. **Close your eyes.** Visualize the old memory clearly—debt notices, calls from collectors, the moment of shame or regret.
2. **Breathe in slowly for 4 counts.** Hold for 4. Exhale for 8.
3. **Now visualize a bright silver flash.** Say aloud (or in your mind):

"This is not who I am. This is a closed mission file."

4.Replace the scene with a new image: you, debt-free, confident, wealthy, calm.

Do this daily for 7 days. You're not ignoring reality—you're **reprogramming your nervous system** to stop fearing the past.

Phase 3: Rebuild the File – Abundance Implant

After a neuralyze, agents implant a new memory to stabilize the subject. You must do the same—implant *abundance code* to replace scarcity.

Write your new financial identity:

- "I manage money with precision and calm."
- "My income grows even in silence."
- "I am not behind. I am rebuilding in stealth."

Then act from this identity daily. Not when you're rich—**now**. Live like the agent you're becoming.

Phase 4: Erase Debt with Tactical Silence

Now, let's talk strategy. You're going to pay off debt like a covert agent—quietly, efficiently, and with zero emotional leakage.

1. The Financial Blackout Strategy (Eliminate Emotional Overspending)

- Freeze all impulse spending channels—delete apps, unsubscribe from marketing emails, and block spending triggers.
- Create a 30-day "financial shadow zone": no unplanned purchases, no flexing, no ego buys.

2. Micro-Mission Payments

Forget the avalanche vs. snowball debate. You're not snow. You're *precision.*

- Choose the debt that compromises your mobility or security first (e.g., car loan, high-interest credit card).
- Create a **micro-mission**: Pay an extra $50/week toward that debt using income from the shadows.
- Every time you pay, write: "Mission neutralized." Then delete the transaction email.

3. No Evidence Method (Emotional Closure)

Once a debt is paid, do something symbolic:

- Delete the payment account from your apps
- Burn the final notice
- Transfer that monthly amount into your **Freedom Fund**

Never revisit it again. **The file is closed.**

Phase 5: Operate in Financial Amnesia (Don't Recreate the Pattern)

The true Neuralyzer effect isn't forgetting—it's *not repeating*.

After your reset, implement stealth systems to protect your new abundance:

- **Auto-withdraw savings** the moment money hits your account (invisible income tactic)
- **Create a Decoy Budget** for public consumption, while your real budget operates in silence
- **Use card cloaking tools** like virtual bank cards to prevent overspending
- **Monitor emotional spending triggers** weekly with a "stealth debrief"

Ask: *Was that purchase for the mission... or for my ego?*

Bonus: Use Shadow Income to Pay Off Debt Anonymously

One of the best ways to erase debt?
Use income no one knows about.

- Take earnings from digital products, POD merch, or freelance gigs
- Funnel it into debt payments without touching your main account
- Never announce the progress—just *delete the debt silently*

When you build income from the shadows, **you remove the emotional toll of repayment** because no one's watching, waiting, or judging.

Final Neuralyzer Truth: You Are Not Your Past Ledger

Your debt isn't who you are.

It's a system you were placed inside.

But now you know how to disappear from it.

The Neuralyzer Method isn't just about paying off balances—it's about erasing the grip debt had on your identity and *reinstalling the agent you were meant to become.*

Suit up.

Flash the past.

And walk into your future like it was always yours.

Because it is.

Chapter 6: The Invisible Wallet

How to Store, Move, and Grow Money Without Drawing Attention

In the Men in Black universe, agents don't walk around with bulky wallets or jingling change. Their identities are wiped. Their transactions are off-grid. Their tools? Streamlined, encrypted, and untraceable. While civilians worry about overdraft fees and card skimming, MiB agents operate financially in ways that leave no trail—and no vulnerabilities.

You need the same strategy.

Welcome to the **Invisible Wallet**—a system designed not just to store and move your money efficiently, but to do so without broadcasting your net worth, triggering systems that monitor spending, or inviting unnecessary attention from predators (digital or human).

In a world where surveillance capitalism, data leaks, and financial profiling are rampant, your **privacy is your greatest financial asset.**

The Core Principle: Wealth That Can't Be Tracked Can't Be Targeted

You don't have to be wealthy yet to need protection.

In fact, the moment you begin building wealth, you become a target:

- Of digital scams
- Of greedy relatives
- Of toxic partners
- Of financial institutions that profile and prey

The Invisible Wallet strategy teaches you to:

- Store wealth discreetly
- Move money securely
- Grow wealth through layered, unexposed channels

You're not hiding. You're **fortifying**.

The Three Compartments of the Invisible Wallet

Like a triple-locked briefcase, your money should be compartmentalized for maximum protection and utility. Here's the agent-grade breakdown:

Compartment 1: The Surface Wallet (Visible & Legal)

This is the only part of your finances that should be visible to banks, employers, landlords, and public-facing platforms.

Purpose: Appear normal, meet daily obligations, provide plausible deniability.

Contents:

- One checking account for bills and deposits
- One savings account with 1–2 months of expenses (just enough to look "safe")
- Public-facing debit card or digital wallet (e.g., Apple Pay, Venmo)

Rules:

- Never use this wallet for high-value purchases or investments
- Keep balances moderate—enough to satisfy financial gatekeepers
- Always transfer excess funds *out* after payday (into Compartment 2)

Agent Tip: Think of this like your "cover story." It exists to function, not to *hold* wealth.

Compartment 2: The Shadow Wallet (Hidden & Strategic)

This is where your true net worth begins.

Purpose: Hold cash reserves, conduct private investments, and grow assets without institutional eyes.

Contents:

- Online-only banks with privacy protections (Ally, Axos, Revolut, etc.)
- Business accounts under your LLC or trust
- Physical cash reserve (stored safely at home in a fireproof, waterproof lockbox)
- Crypto wallets (cold wallets preferred)
- High-yield savings accounts that are disconnected from your main bank

Rules:

- No linking to social media, PayPal, or retail platforms
- Use aliases, LLC names, or project code names for transactions
- Rotate which accounts receive money to avoid traceable patterns

Agent Tip: Fund this wallet using income from your shadow operations—print-on-demand, affiliate links, ghostwriting, royalties, etc. **This is your engine, not your mask.**

Compartment 3: The Ghost Wallet (Exit-Only Assets)

This compartment is for worst-case scenarios, long-term sovereignty, and off-grid wealth that survives collapse, surveillance, or conflict.

Purpose: Become untraceable. Rebuild from scratch. Exit any system, any time.

Contents:

- Physical precious metals (silver, gold, platinum) stored in non-bank safes
- Cold storage crypto wallets (hardware wallets like Ledger or Trezor)
- Prepaid travel cards or digital assets stored offshore
- Barterable goods: tools, emergency rations, rare items
- Land titles or deeds not linked to your name but to a holding company or trust

Rules:

- This wallet never interacts with the digital world
- No subscriptions, no transfers, no receipts
- Access only during complete extraction missions (job loss, political unrest, or personal crisis)

Agent Tip: Treat this like a black site. You don't even tell yourself about it unless the mission demands it.

Transaction Stealth: How to Move Money Without Flash

1. **Round Amount Transfers = Risk**
   Transfer *non-round* numbers. $479.63 is less suspicious than $500.00.
2. **Use Bridges**
   Move money through intermediary apps like Cash App or Wise, but always clear the balance. Don't let money linger in third-party platforms.
3. **Rename Transactions**
   Some banks allow you to label transactions. Use innocuous terms like "Supplies" or "Training" instead of "Savings."
4. **Time Your Transfers Strategically**
   Send money late at night or early morning to avoid triggering automated bank alerts or fraud flags.
5. **Avoid Predictable Patterns**
   Don't always transfer money on the same day or at the same interval. Patterns are how systems profile behavior.

Invisible Wallet Growth Tactics

Now that your wallet is hidden, you need to **grow your assets without growing your exposure.**

1. **Use Business Entities to Build Credit**
   Your personal score stays protected while your LLC builds a new identity.
2. **Buy Assets in Other Names**
   Property under an LLC. Domains under aliases. Stock portfolios held in trusts. This protects against lawsuits, taxes, and nosy relatives.
3. **Invest in Quiet Assets**
   - Royalty rights (music, books, IP)
   - Land in rural or low-regulation areas
   - Peer-to-peer lending (under pseudonym accounts)
   - Real-world items that appreciate (tools, equipment, storage units)
4. **Leverage Debt Only Through Shielded Channels**
   If you must use credit, route it through a business or a secured card not tied to your full profile.

Emotional Discipline: Don't Flash the Wallet

You don't need to show people you're winning. That's how agents get compromised.

Signs you're slipping into exposure:

- Bragging about earnings on social media
- Making large purchases before you've solidified exit wealth
- Sharing investment wins with people who don't contribute to your success

If you must celebrate, do it in private. True power needs no parade.

Conclusion: Protect the Core, Disappear the Rest

Your wallet isn't just where you store money.

It's a map of your behavior. A record of your values. A target, if you're not careful.

So restructure it. Encrypt it. Shield it.

Let the world see a calm agent in a black suit with just enough money to get by.

Meanwhile—your real fortune moves silently, multiplies in the dark, and waits for the right moment to activate.

Because wealth isn't power until it's **protected.**

And when it's invisible?

It becomes unstoppable.

Chapter 7: Silence Is Leverage

Why Saying Less Builds More Power, Profit, and Protection

In the *Men in Black* world, silence isn't awkward—it's **strategic**. Agents don't boast, overshare, or explain themselves. They let others talk, observe everything, and speak only when the mission requires it. That silence? It's not just cool—it's tactical.

In the financial world, silence is just as powerful.

The most successful, sovereign individuals understand that silence creates leverage. The less you reveal, the more you control. The quieter your moves, the fewer obstacles you invite. In this chapter, we'll unlock the full power of strategic silence—not just in speech, but in your behavior, your business, your brand, and your investments.

This is how you **build a fortune without becoming a target.** This is how you become **a ghost with influence.**

The Myth of Loud Success

Modern culture worships visibility. Post your wins. Share your income. Document every milestone. But what most people don't see is that:

- **Loud wealth attracts predators.**
- **Loud success invites sabotage.**
- **Loud ambition becomes predictable.**

It's easy to attack what you can see.
But you can't sabotage what you don't understand.

Silence as a Wealth Strategy

1. Silence Protects Your Blueprint

The moment you speak your goals aloud to the wrong person, they become vulnerable. Negative energy, jealousy, distraction, or even "helpful" criticism can **weaken your focus** or kill your momentum.

What people don't know, they can't distort.

Your business model, your investments, your side hustles—these are **classified operations.** They don't belong in group chats, family dinners, or office banter.

2. Silence Builds Anticipation and Respect

Loud people are dismissed as attention-seekers. Silent people? They're **watched.** They're assumed to know more than they show.

In negotiation, sales, and even friendship, silence gives you leverage:

- The person who talks less **controls the pace**.
- The one who listens more **gathers intelligence**.
- The agent who stays calm under pressure **wins without force.**

3. Silence Grants You Freedom to Pivot

The loud path traps you in your image. If everyone knows you as the "crypto guy," what happens when crypto crashes and you want to pivot to real estate?

But when you've kept your plans close to your chest, you can **change direction without explanation**. You're never boxed into an identity you've overshared.

Silence makes you agile.

And **agility is more valuable than accuracy** in volatile markets.

Tactical Applications of Silence

Now let's put silence into real-world financial practice:

Business & Side Hustles

- **Use pseudonyms or brand names** instead of your personal identity
- **Never announce your business until it earns consistently**
- **Avoid mentorship addiction**—too much advice causes confusion and second-guessing
- **Let your customers discover you**—organic reputation is stronger than paid advertising

Agent Tip: Launch your first five products without telling a soul. Refine in silence. Scale in stealth. Profit in peace.

Income Streams

- Keep your income diversified but **never listed publicly**
- When asked what you "do for work," have a neutral, vague answer ready (e.g., "digital consulting," "content strategy," "logistics")
- Avoid discussing earnings with friends, family, or acquaintances

Money discussed is money targeted.
Money hidden is money protected.

Relationships & Family

- Don't loan money. Don't talk about what you've made.
- Keep boundaries tight: the fewer people who see your finances, the fewer financial emergencies you're pulled into
- Don't announce moves like a relocation, land purchase, or new opportunity until **after it's done**

Agent Tip: Build your escape plan in silence. Let the announcement be your absence.

Social Media

- Turn off comments on posts about money or success
- Never brag about purchases or income
- Don't post screenshots of earnings or dashboards
- Avoid "financial flex" content—it trains algorithms to feed you comparisons, envy, and attacks

Your account isn't a trophy case.
It's a shield.

The Economics of Silence

Let's break it down:

Silent Action	Wealth Impact
Quietly investing monthly	Builds long-term wealth without pressure
Not disclosing your net worth	Reduces manipulation, protects privacy
Declining to share business ideas	Keeps competitors in the dark
Operating under an alias or LLC	Protects identity, reduces liability
Refusing to brag about wins	Increases mystique and negotiation power

Your silence compounds like interest.
And unlike loud spending—it never depreciates.

When to Speak (Strategically)

Silence doesn't mean passivity. It means **timing.**

Speak only when:

- A deal must be closed, and silence has raised your value
- You're negotiating, and a few well-placed words tilt the balance
- You're teaching from results—not theories
- You've already completed the mission

When you speak, it should be:

- **Precise**
- **Measured**
- **Unignorable**

Speak like an agent filing a report—**only when required, and always with control.**

Conclusion: The Quieter You Are, The More You Own

True wealth? It's not loud.
It doesn't need a parade, applause, or permission.

It grows behind closed doors.
It compounds in the shadows.
And it walks into rooms with presence—not noise.

Silence isn't weakness.
It's the ultimate leverage.

So the next time someone asks, "How's your money doing?"
Smile. Nod. Say, "I'm doing alright."

Meanwhile—your empire grows in silence.
And they'll never see it coming.

Because you don't need to speak when the **briefcase speaks for itself.**

Chapter 8: The Black Briefcase Protocol

How to Design Your Personal Wealth Command Center

The black briefcase in *Men in Black* isn't just a prop—it's a symbol of absolute readiness. Inside that sleek, unassuming case is everything an agent needs: tools, tech, weapons, data, and codes. It's not chaotic. It's not cluttered. It's **intentional, essential, and lethal in its precision**.

Now imagine applying that same philosophy to your finances.

This chapter teaches you how to build your own **Black Briefcase Protocol**—a centralized, structured, and silent wealth system. It's not a literal briefcase (though you could make one); it's a method of organizing every aspect of your financial life into one clear, mobile-ready command center.

If your money, mission documents, goals, income streams, passwords, and strategic backups aren't easy to access, update, or extract at a moment's notice—**you're not ready for the field.**

By the end of this chapter, you'll have a personalized protocol that makes you immune to confusion, chaos, or collapse.

The Core Principle: Chaos Is the Enemy of Control

Disorganized finances are the enemy of wealth. If you can't locate your accounts, track your expenses, explain your strategy, or act quickly in a crisis—then you're vulnerable.

Agents aren't just prepared. They're overprepared, underseen, and always in control.

Your mission: **build a Black Briefcase system so effective, it could survive a wipeout—and reboot your life within 24 hours.**

What Goes Into the Black Briefcase Protocol?

There are 6 key compartments every agent-grade wealth command system must include:

Compartment 1: Mission Ledger (Your Wealth Map)

This is your financial command document—a top-level dashboard of everything you own, owe, and earn.

Contents:

- Net worth tracker (assets – liabilities)
- List of all accounts (banking, investment, crypto, business)
- List of monthly income sources (side hustles, royalties, salary, etc.)
- List of recurring expenses with due dates

Tool Options:

- Notion or Obsidian vault
- Encrypted Excel/Google Sheets
- Physical ledger in a fireproof safe
- Custom app dashboard (e.g., Monarch, Tiller, YNAB)

Agent Tip: Use **code names** for sensitive accounts. Never label a tab “Bitcoin Wallet” or “Escape Fund.” Use neutral terms like “Project Echo” or “Zone 7.”

Compartment 2: The Silent Budget (Operational Flow Plan)

Forget chaotic spreadsheets with 75 categories. This is your **agent-style, streamlined budget**:

Categories:

- Essentials (housing, food, transport)
- Growth (education, investing, skills)
- Buffer (emergency, backup, off-grid)
- Expansion (side hustles, ventures, gear)
- Containment (luxury, leisure, flex)

Set spending limits, automate transfers, and treat your budget like a **weapons loadout**—everything has a job. Anything not assigned is dead weight.

Agent Tip: Automate 80% of this flow. Manual decisions = vulnerability.

Compartment 3: Asset Vault (Everything You Own That Grows)

Your briefcase should track every income-producing or appreciating asset:

- Stocks, ETFs, REITs
- Rental property, land, digital real estate (domains, ad revenue)
- Crypto and hard wallets
- Royalties (books, music, content)
- Cash equivalents (precious metals, stablecoins, cash reserves)

For each, include:

- Purchase date and value
- Access credentials (stored separately in encrypted format)
- Current value and growth target
- Strategy for exit or scale

Agent Tip: Include at least one **stealth asset**—something earning while disconnected from your name.

Compartment 4: Escape Infrastructure (Emergency Protocol)

This is your **go-bag in digital form**. What if everything collapsed tomorrow?

Include:

- Emergency contacts (bank, lawyer, accountant, tech support)
- Digital backups of ID, passport, business licenses, EINs
- Password list (stored offline or in 2FA-protected app like Bitwarden)
- Backup crypto seed phrases (handwritten, fireproof)
- Pre-made templates: resignation letter, move-out checklist, relocation budget

Agent Tip: Test your emergency extraction quarterly. Can you "leave" your current job, account, or address in 48 hours with zero panic? If not, your protocol is incomplete.

Compartment 5: Influence Folder (Strategic Communication Tools)

Even covert agents need to **transmit messages that control perception.**

Include:

- Pre-written cold outreach scripts (for business, affiliates, advisors)
- Exit scripts (for jobs, partnerships, toxic relationships)
- Your brand bio and elevator pitch (for stealth business ventures)
- Mission statements for key projects (side hustles, digital products, ventures)

Agent Tip: Keep a file titled **"The 90-Second Script"** —a universal verbal briefing you can give on who you are, what you do, and what you offer in a controlled, agent-like way.

Compartment 6: Silent Income Tracker (Command + Control)
Track every cent that enters your system, from every stream:

- Daily: Digital product sales, affiliate commissions, freelance gigs
- Weekly: Royalty payments, client work, platform payouts
- Monthly: Book sales, investments, rent, or dividends
- Quarterly: Growth benchmarks, bonuses, tax savings

Track *where*, *when*, and *how fast* each income source grows.

Agent Tip: Use a **color-coded alert system**: Green = stable income. Yellow = slowing or dependent. Red = dying stream. Black = stealth-only (invisible to public).

Optional Physical Briefcase (For Elite Preparedness)
Want to go full MiB mode? Build a **physical Black Briefcase** with:

- Burner phone with encrypted SIM
- Flash drive with encrypted backup files
- $1,000 in mixed currency (small bills)
- Portable Wi-Fi device or hotspot SIM
- Passport or ID photocopy
- Printed protocol checklist and maps

This briefcase is for **total reboot missions**—when digital isn't enough, and you need to vanish.

Maintaining Your Black Briefcase Protocol

1. **Weekly Tactical Review (15 min)**
    - Update income streams
    - Review expenses
    - Scan for vulnerabilities
2. **Monthly Intel Sync (30–60 min)**
    - Recalculate net worth
    - Reassign budget flow
    - Adjust asset allocation
3. **Quarterly Field Test**
    - Practice financial extraction: could you shift your base of operations or income in under 3 days?
4. **Annual Protocol Refresh**
    - Audit all accounts, assets, and passwords
    - Rename or rotate compartments
    - Add new streams and retire dead ones

Conclusion: Be Your Own Financial Command Center

Your financial life isn't random.
It's not a spreadsheet.
It's not a mess of apps and numbers.

It's a **mission**.
And you are the **operative** in charge of executing it with precision.

When you create your Black Briefcase Protocol:

- You never forget where your money is.
- You never wonder what your next move is.
- You never panic in a crisis.

You control the data.
You control the narrative.
And you control your outcome.

Because true wealth doesn't just grow in silence.
It's **commanded** from the shadows—with one briefcase, and one master: *you.*

Chapter 9: The Cloaking Strategy

How to Protect Wealth from Predators, Parasites, and Public Systems

In the *Men in Black* universe, cloaking is standard protocol. From spaceships to alien refugees, anything worth protecting is hidden. The moment you're seen, you're vulnerable. And in the world of money, it's exactly the same.

The more visible your wealth, the more exposed you are to:

- Legal attacks
- Tax audits
- Financial leeches
- Jealous peers
- Opportunistic family members
- Predatory relationships
- Corporate surveillance
- Government overreach

That's why this chapter introduces the **Cloaking Strategy**—a comprehensive system for protecting your wealth, income streams, and identity through strategic concealment. You're not hiding because you're doing something wrong. You're cloaking because you're doing something **valuable**—and value attracts danger.

If you want to survive as a silent millionaire, **you must master the art of being rich without becoming a target.**

The Core Principle: Protection Before Expansion

The average person builds wealth first, then worries about protecting it later.

But agents know better. They shield before they scale. Before you earn your first $100K or $1M, your systems should already be hardened, disguised, and legally protected.

"Don't announce your treasure map before you've buried the gold."
—The Cloaking Doctrine

Threats to Your Financial Safety

Let's identify the most common "enemies of silence":

1. Digital Predators

- Hackers targeting payment platforms, wallets, and personal data.
- Leaked data on public Wi-Fi or unsecured apps.

2. Relational Parasites

- Friends or family who expect access to your money.
- Partners who weaponize financial information in emotional conflicts.

3. Legal Snipers

- People filing frivolous lawsuits after seeing visible signs of wealth.
- Ex-partners, ex-friends, or ex-business collaborators seeking revenge or a payout.

4. Institutional Watchdogs

- Governments tracking large or irregular transactions.
- Banks reporting deposits or withdrawals over certain thresholds.

The Cloaking Strategy Framework

This strategy has five levels, each one building on the next. As your wealth grows, **so does your level of concealment.**

Level 1: Personal Cloaking – Obscure Your Identity

Goal: Decouple your full name from every financial operation.

Tactics:

- Use business entities (LLCs, trusts) as the face of your operations.
- Buy digital assets (domains, websites) under your company, not your personal name.
- Register for tools using a business email, not a Gmail tied to your full name.
- Use a VPN, privacy browsers (Brave), and tools like DuckDuckGo to reduce digital footprint.

Agent Tip: *Use a neutral alias for forums, investment platforms, and public profiles. You don't need to lie—you need to separate.*

Level 2: Transaction Cloaking – Mask Your Financial Behavior

Goal: Prevent surveillance of how you earn, spend, or move your money.

Tactics:

- Funnel income into a business account first, then pay yourself a fixed "salary."
- Use non-round numbers for transfers (e.g., $462.91 instead of $500).
- Withdraw cash in smaller increments, and never on a schedule.
- Split transactions between different platforms (e.g., PayPal, Stripe, Venmo, Zelle).
- Don't let multiple income streams touch the same account.

Agent Tip: Avoid showing patterns. The more irregular your movements, the harder it is to profile you.

Level 3: Relationship Cloaking – Withhold Financial Access
Goal: Limit who knows what—and who can access what.
Tactics:

- Never co-sign. Ever.
- Never give friends, family, or partners your login credentials—*no matter how much you trust them.*
- Use prepaid debit cards for shared expenses.
- Keep emergency funds completely separate and unshared.
- Have a private "clean break" account: a silent reserve that no one else knows exists.

Agent Tip: If someone gets angry when you set financial boundaries, they were planning to breach them.

Level 4: Asset Cloaking – Hide What You Own

Goal: Legally own and control assets without making yourself an easy target.

Tactics:

- Own rental properties or land through LLCs.
- Keep crypto in cold wallets—*never stored on exchanges.*
- Use trusts for long-term assets (especially in estate planning).
- Separate personal assets from business operations with legal fire-walls.
- Store precious metals in secure, off-site depositories, not your home.

Agent Tip: Your name should appear on as few public records as possible. Let your *entities* do the work.

Level 5: Exit Cloaking – Disappear Financially When Needed

Goal: Leave a system—job, country, city, platform—without sacrificing control of your wealth.

Tactics:

- Have an "off-grid" emergency plan (see Chapter 4: Emergency Exit Wealth).
- Hold passports or access to alternate jurisdictions with favorable privacy laws.
- Store key documents, backups, and funds in encrypted drives or private vaults.
- Preload prepaid debit cards and crypto wallets in case you need to travel or flee.
- Keep accounts open in multiple institutions to avoid single-point failure.

Agent Tip: Think like a spy. **Always have an escape route and a relocation budget.**

What Cloaking Is NOT

- It's not illegal. (You're not hiding income from taxes—just keeping it off public radar.)
- It's not paranoia. (It's smart, strategic, and protective.)
- It's not antisocial. (You can love people without financially exposing yourself to them.)
- It's not selfish. (Boundaries preserve generosity—because you give from surplus, not fear.)

Tools for the Modern Cloak

- **LLC Formation Sites:** ZenBusiness, Northwest Registered Agent, LegalZoom
- **Anonymous Browsing:** Brave Browser, Tor, ProtonVPN
- **Encrypted Storage:** ProtonDrive, Tresorit, IronKey USBs
- **Digital Banks with Privacy:** Revolut, N26, Wise (multi-currency for travel)
- **Virtual Cards:** Privacy.com, Eco, or your bank's card-cloaking tool
- **Cold Wallets:** Ledger Nano, Trezor, Arculus
- **Digital Asset Protection:** Docusign + Blockchain records

Conclusion: Cloak What Counts

Your wealth is like a spaceship. It's sleek, powerful, valuable—and **fragile if unprotected**.

Don't let outsiders dock without authorization.
Don't broadcast your flight path.
Don't leave your access codes in plain view.

Cloak what counts.
Let the world see only what you want it to.

Because the richest agents don't flaunt.
They vanish—with everything they built fully intact.

And when the lights come back on,
they're five moves ahead... already cloaked again.

Chapter 10: The Agent's Legacy Plan

Building Wealth That Outlives You Without Leaving a Trace of Chaos

Men in Black agents don't retire. They vanish. No farewell speeches, no public goodbyes—just a silent transition, their work encoded into mission logs, their impact felt but never announced. No mess. No confusion. Just **clean, complete closure**.

Your financial life should be no different.

When most people think of legacy, they think of inheritance, wills, or estates. But that's *civilian thinking*. Agents operate differently. Legacy isn't about what you leave **behind**—it's about what you leave **ready**. It's not about wealth transfer. It's about **mission continuity** without chaos.

In this final core chapter, we establish your **Agent's Legacy Plan**—a detailed, private, and powerfully structured strategy for ensuring that your wealth, ideas, systems, and values **outlive you**, even if your name disappears.

Because the most dangerous thing you can do is build an empire... and then leave no map for what comes next.

The Core Principle: Legacy Without Leakage
Your wealth isn't just money. It's:

- The systems you built
- The businesses you launched
- The people you've protected
- The assets you've acquired
- The missions only you could complete

But without a clean legacy structure, all of that can be lost to:

- Probate court delays
- Tax seizures
- Family infighting
- Digital lockouts
- Legal ambiguity
- Greedy institutions

An agent doesn't let the mission fall apart when they're gone.
They encode it. Protect it. Pass it on without friction.

The 4 Levels of the Agent's Legacy Plan

Level 1: Legacy Mindset Reset – You Are Not Immortal

Agents plan for disappearance at any time. Civilians wait too long and leave confusion.

Ask yourself:

- If I disappeared today, would my finances collapse?
- Would my income streams stop?
- Would my digital business be locked forever?
- Would my loved ones know how to access anything?

The Legacy Plan begins with **acceptance and accountability**. You don't need to be old. You need to be **ready**.

Level 2: The Silent Vault – Centralizing What You Own

You need a private, protected, and consolidated system for all wealth-related data. This is your **Legacy Vault**.

What goes in:

- Master list of all income streams and business accounts
- Domain registrations, login credentials, crypto wallets, royalties
- Passwords (stored in a password manager or printed in an encrypted location)
- Legal documents: birth certificate, SSN, passport, ID, insurance
- LLC paperwork, EINs, trademarks, trust documents
- Contact info for financial allies (lawyer, accountant, executor, tax advisor)

Where to store it:

- Encrypted USB drive stored in a fireproof safe
- Cloud-based vault with dual access (e.g., Proton Drive, Dropbox with 2FA)
- Safety deposit box with documented access
- Physical backup copy in a sealed envelope, labeled *"Mission Access – Open Only If Necessary"*

Agent Tip: Label your vault clearly with simple instructions: "In the event of disappearance or death, contact [X]. This file contains access to all mission-critical systems."

Level 3: Legal Echoes – Ensuring Your Wealth Transfers Quietly

Every agent needs **legal shadow systems** that allow wealth to pass on **without courts or conflict**.

1. Living Trust

- Avoids probate entirely
- Allows assets to transfer instantly
- Can contain property, stocks, cash, crypto, and even business shares
- Invisible to the public (unlike wills)

2. Pour-Over Will

- Acts as a backup that funnels any missed assets into the trust
- Used to protect the "overflow" and maintain control

3. Power of Attorney

- Grants a trusted person the ability to act on your behalf if you're incapacitated
- Must be precise: limit access only to what's necessary

4. Healthcare Directive

- Decides your medical treatment protocols if you're unable to speak
- Keeps vultures out of life-or-death decisions

Agent Tip: If you have a digital empire, designate a **Digital Executor**—someone trained to access and manage online accounts, platforms, and business systems.

Level 4: Succession Programming – Training Your Shadow Operatives

Legacy isn't just paperwork. It's **transmission of intelligence**.

Ask:

- Who will run your systems if you vanish?
- Who understands your brand, your customers, your voice?
- Who can activate dormant income streams or sell your content?

Options:

- Train a trusted family member or friend through written SOPs (standard operating procedures)
- Pre-record walkthroughs of your backend systems (store in encrypted vault)
- Hire a business continuity specialist to audit your systems for "vanish-proofing"
- Schedule check-ins with your successor every 6 months (even if they don't know why yet)

Bonus Tactic: Leave behind a *"Legacy Activation Folder"* with step-by-step instructions. Think of it like a **mission file** for those who come after you.

Digital Legacy: What Happens to Your Online Presence?

Social media, YouTube, KDP, Etsy, Stripe, PayPal—these platforms can freeze accounts after inactivity or death. Prevent this:

- Name a **Legacy Contact** in Meta/Apple/Facebook settings
- Include login info in your vault
- Keep email and 2FA systems active and documented
- Use business bank accounts (not personal ones) to avoid lockouts upon death
- Set up auto-forwarding on your main emails so nothing is missed

Agent Tip: **Write a final public message** in advance (e.g., for a website or pinned tweet). Your legacy doesn't have to vanish with you—it can trigger one last coded broadcast.

What Legacy Really Means (Agent Edition)

It's not about leaving behind a mess of passwords, legal fights, or panicked calls to banks.

It's about:

- Leaving peace instead of pressure
- Passing control, not chaos
- Quietly continuing your mission even in your absence
- Ensuring your empire serves others even if you're not present

The best legacy?

A system that doesn't need you to function.

Final Cloaked Directive: Disappear Clean

Before you disappear:

- Confirm your Vault is updated
- Confirm your legal documents are active
- Confirm someone trustworthy knows where to look
- Confirm your income streams don't depend on your presence
- Confirm your mission is encoded, accessible, and protected

Then rest easy—because your work continues without you.

Conclusion: The Legacy Is the System

You are not the business.
You are not the brand.
You are not even the money.

You are the **architect of the system**.

And when the time comes, that system will activate, echo, and endure—without noise, without drama, and without traceable fingerprints.

That's the Agent's Legacy.

Silently built.
Flawlessly transferred.
Never forgotten.

Chapter 11: The Suit-and-Shadows Strategy

How to Look Ordinary While Living Exceptionally

Men in Black agents are invisible in plain sight. Black suit. Clean shoes. Calm demeanor. No bling, no bragging, no obvious signs of authority. And yet—they have access to secrets that control galaxies. That's not just style. That's strategy.

You don't build wealth by standing out. You build it by **blending in**—until it's too late for anyone to stop you.

In this chapter, we'll walk through the **Suit-and-Shadows Strategy**—a blueprint for living a life of exceptional wealth, freedom, and power while **appearing completely ordinary to everyone around you**. This is the key to avoiding envy, theft, interference, and manipulation in a world obsessed with appearances.

Because when you master invisibility, no one sees your moves.

And when no one sees your moves, **you always stay ahead.**

The Core Principle: Stop Signaling Wealth

Wealth is not what you show.
It's what you *control* without exposing it.

"The loudest one in the room is the weakest one."
— Frank Lucas, *American Gangster*

You don't want to look rich. You want to look **unremarkable.** The goal is **social camouflage**: living well, earning massively, and owning systems—while **never becoming a target.**

Why Ordinary Appearance Is Ultimate Protection

In today's world:

- Flash invites theft
- Bragging invites lawsuits
- Status symbols attract scrutiny
- Online presence becomes evidence
- Even "friends" can turn predatory when they know too much

But the person in plain clothes who never overshares?

They move freely.
They avoid jealousy.
They never invite attack.
They control wealth **quietly**.

That's the **Suit-and-Shadows Strategy** in motion.

The 5 Rules of the Suit-and-Shadows Strategy

Rule 1: Dress With Tactical Neutrality
You don't have to look broke. You just have to look **controlled.**

- Invest in **neutral, quality clothing** that doesn't scream brand names.
- Stick to **dark, clean palettes** (gray, navy, black, white).
- Avoid flashy logos, designer bags, or anything that triggers recognition.
- Blend in with your environment—never try to "dominate" a room visually.
- Upgrade fabrics, not flash. Comfort and durability are quiet signs of wealth.

Agent Tip: A $60 jacket that fits like a glove says more than a $3,000 one with logos all over it. Fit = command.

Rule 2: Speak With Low-Signal Language
Verbal flash is just as dangerous as visual flash.

- Don't talk about money. Not your earnings, your deals, or your assets.
- Never use phrases like "I made six figures last month" or "I'm crushing it."
- If asked what you do, give **vague but respectable** answers like:
    - "I do consulting."
    - "I manage systems."
    - "I'm in content strategy."
- Avoid revealing numbers, timelines, or proprietary methods.

Why? Because once they know what you have, **they'll calculate how to get it.**

Rule 3: Buy Assets, Not Applause

Many people buy things to be seen. You will buy things to **be free**.
Skip:

- Luxury watches
- Sports cars
- Loud vacations
- Obvious tech toys

Invest in:

- Land and real estate (especially income-producing)
- Equipment that automates your income
- Intellectual property (books, media, patents, courses)
- Private training and elite networks

Agent Tip: Don't "look" like a millionaire. **Move like one.**

Rule 4: Hide in the Algorithms
Your digital shadow is bigger than you realize.

- Avoid tagging expensive locations in real-time (hotels, flights, restaurants)
- Never show purchases, dashboards, or financial software in photos
- Limit your followers' ability to monitor your habits—don't post daily routines
- Use neutral handles or burner profiles for high-level research or transactions
- Scrub metadata from documents and photos (time, location, device info)

The more the algorithm knows, the more others will find.
Suit-and-Shadows means: **low engagement, high movement.**

Rule 5: Master the Gray Man Technique

The "Gray Man" is a military espionage tactic:

Be so boring and average that you're **ignored by default**.

This doesn't mean you have no style or presence. It means you **choose when to appear powerful.**

How to master it:

- Keep a composed body language: never frantic, always observant
- Don't share opinions unless strategically advantageous
- Let others underestimate you
- Never correct someone's assumptions about your finances
- Observe patterns. Control tempo. Move when no one's watching.

Remember: You want *freedom*, not *attention*. Attention is the tax on visibility. **Freedom is the reward for silence.**

Creating a Life That Looks Simple But Feeds Power

Here's a practical day-in-the-life of a Suit-and-Shadows operative:

Surface Behavior	Hidden Strategy
Drives a 5-year-old car	Owns land, cash-flow rentals, and crypto nodes
Orders basic coffee	Writes under 4 pseudonyms on 6 platforms
Lives in a modest neighborhood	Has offshore trusts and diversified assets
Says "I work in digital operations"	Owns 3 passive businesses generating 5 figures
Wears black, navy, and white clothes	Custom tailored, built to last for a decade

You are **a phantom of excellence**.
To the world? Simple.
To your bank account? Strategic.
To your legacy? Lethal.

The Power of Being Underestimated

This strategy is not just protection. It's **leverage.**

When people think you're "average," they:

- Don't compete with you
- Don't beg from you
- Don't interfere with your plans
- Don't study your movements
- Don't expect resistance when you pivot

So when you finally launch a new product, buy land, move to another country, or retire early?

They're shocked.

But you're already gone.

Because you lived in the shadows.

And ruled from the silence.

Conclusion: Look Basic. Operate Brilliantly.

You don't need validation.

You don't need applause.

You don't need to be loud to be legendary.

You just need:

- Quiet power
- Invisible systems
- Absolute control
- And the confidence to **let others underestimate you.**

The Suit-and-Shadows Strategy isn't about hiding.

It's about **winning while no one's watching.**

So button your coat.

Lower your voice.

And keep walking.

Because the richest agent in the room is never the one bragging.
It's the one blending in—already five steps ahead.

Chapter 12: The Silence Protocol

Becoming Untouchable in a World That Can't Track You

This is the final chapter.

Not because the mission ends here—but because **you disappear beyond the need for instruction.**

By now, you've built the infrastructure. You've layered your defenses. You've created quiet income, armored your identity, coded your legacy, cloaked your movements, and vanished into the system like smoke through wires.

But there's one final protocol left.

It's not about building wealth.

It's about becoming **immune to interference**—from systems, from people, from your own past.

This is the **Silence Protocol**: a total life integration of power, protection, purpose, and invisibility. It's the moment you stop reacting to the world and start *moving above it.*

When this protocol is complete, no one can audit your mission.

No one can reroute your path.

No one can sabotage what they cannot detect.

You're no longer chasing wealth.

You've become **wealth.**

The Silence Protocol Defined

The Silence Protocol is **not passive**. It's not about being quiet to avoid conflict.

It's a *discipline* that:

- Shields your vision
- Controls your frequency
- Alters how others perceive your presence
- Extracts you from every system of surveillance, sabotage, and distraction

It turns your entire life into a **ghost network** of influence and income—fully active, but never traceable.

You no longer need to speak to be heard.

You no longer need to fight to win.

You no longer need to exist in their system to master it.

The 7 Seals of the Silence Protocol

1. Sealed Identity

- You are not your job title.
- You are not your LinkedIn.
- You are not your follower count.

You are a **multi-entity intelligence system** wrapped in a civilian disguise.

You operate under:

- Codenames (online and off)
- Legal shells (LLCs, trusts)
- Dual citizenships or escape jurisdictions
- Professional aliases for each income stream

People know the name.
They never see the controller.

2. Sealed Intentions

You've stopped announcing your goals.
Because **your outcomes are coded into action—not conversation**.

- Your calendar is encrypted
- Your conversations are layered in non-disclosure
- Your plans unfold without broadcast
- Your pivots happen before anyone can notice

You've weaponized discretion.
You speak only when the result is already complete.

3. Sealed Movements

Your location is a rumor.
Your habits are untrackable.
Your travel is never posted in real-time.

You:

- Use encrypted devices
- Cloak your purchases
- Disable digital breadcrumbs
- Rotate your environment
- Change your rhythm often enough to stay unpredictable

Where you are is never the question.
Where you're *going*—even less so.

4. Sealed Emotions

You no longer bleed in public.
You've stopped giving enemies data through your reactions.

- You listen instead of defend
- You vanish instead of argue
- You smile instead of explain
- You move instead of beg

Your emotions belong to you.
And you've stopped renting them out to situations that don't pay.

5. Sealed Wealth

Your money no longer lives in one account.
It's distributed. Layered. Protected. Invisible.

You:

- Hold assets others don't understand
- Move funds through shadow accounts
- Split income across systems
- Collect royalty streams with no public face
- Store backup wealth outside the reach of borders, banks, or bureaucrats

No one knows where it all is.
But it's all working for you—*24/7, in silence.*

6. Sealed Relationships

You don't share the crown with chaos.

You've:

- Cut loose every emotional liability
- Removed your energy from needy, dramatic, or manipulative people
- Built partnerships on results, not sentiment
- Refused access to those who violated trust once

You no longer confuse love with liability.
Your network is *elite, intentional, and silent.*

7. Sealed Future

The final seal isn't just about today—it's about **outlasting the system**.

You've:

- Structured your legacy for seamless transfer
- Created generational encryption protocols (trusts, vaults, continuity plans)
- Built knowledge that outlives you (books, systems, ghost operations)
- Funded escape routes no one knows exist
- Made peace with being *forgotten by the world—but never outmaneuvered by it*

Your future doesn't need applause.
It needs **infrastructure**. And now, it's done.

Becoming the Phantom Asset

There comes a moment when an agent becomes something more than a worker, more than a name on a document, more than a presence in the room.

They become **an unshakable force** behind systems, strategies, and entire economies—without needing to show up at all.

You are no longer just an entrepreneur.

You're a **phantom asset**—self-sustaining, self-defending, self-expanding.

You don't ask for approval.

You don't ask for help.

You don't ask for credit.

Because **you're not playing their game.**

Conclusion: Vanish Loudly

They will wonder how you:

- Traveled so far
- Built so much
- Escaped so cleanly
- Became so powerful
- And yet… left no trail behind

And the truth is:
You mastered the Silence Protocol.

You built a life that is:

- Quiet in process
- Untraceable in progress
- And undeniable in outcome

Let others chase influence.
Let them perform success.
Let them pose for photos with the empire they haven't built yet.

You?
You already left the building.
The empire runs itself.
And the shadows carry your name.

Because in the end…

The loudest force in the world is not a scream.
It's a whisper that outlasts every voice.
And you've just become that whisper.

Mission complete.
Briefcase closed.
You are now untouchable.

Appendix A – Stealth Wealth Checklist

How to Move Like You're Worth Millions—Quietly

You don't have to flaunt wealth to live richly. In fact, the wealthiest agents move in silence, hidden behind plain clothes, vague language, and layered systems. They blend in—until they've already outmaneuvered everyone in the room.

This checklist is your quick-access **operational blueprint** for maintaining **stealth wealth**: the ability to grow, protect, and enjoy millions without drawing attention, envy, interference, or unnecessary risk.

Use this as your **monthly audit, pre-mission review, or lifestyle recalibration protocol**.

◈ I. Identity Cloaking

Task	Complete?
Use aliases or codenames for online work (freelance, authorship, business projects)	◈
Maintain at least one LLC or business entity not publicly tied to your legal name	◈
Use business or encrypted emails (e.g., ProtonMail) for income and operations	◈
Avoid using your full name on public business platforms (Stripe, Gumroad, etc.)	◈
Separate personal and business social media entirely	◈

⟐ II. Banking & Financial Behavior

Task	Complete?
Have multiple bank accounts across different institutions	⟐
Use at least one online-only, privacy-focused bank (e.g., Revolut, Axos, Wise)	⟐
Store cash reserves in physical form (hidden, fireproof, waterproof)	⟐
Use virtual debit cards for all digital subscriptions and risky purchases	⟐
Transfer income in non-round, irregular amounts (e.g., $439.22 instead of $500)	⟐
Automate transfers to emergency and investment accounts within 24 hours of income	⟐

⯑ III. Digital Silence Protocol

Task	Complete?
Browse using VPN and a private browser (e.g., Brave, Firefox with uBlock)	⯑
Regularly clear browser cookies, cache, and metadata	⯑
Avoid real-time posts of travel, purchases, or locations	⯑
Scrub metadata from images and PDFs before uploading or sharing	⯑
Store important files in encrypted cloud drives with two-factor authentication	⯑
Use a password manager (e.g., Bitwarden, ProtonPass) for all login data	⯑

⟐ IV. Asset Disguise & Diversification

Task	Complete?
Own at least one income-producing asset that's not tied to your legal name	⟐
Hold real estate through an LLC or trust	⟐
Store precious metals in a private location or secure third-party vault	⟐
Maintain cold-storage crypto wallets disconnected from exchanges	⟐
Use royalty income (books, music, content) under pseudonyms	⟐
Keep one shadow income stream separate from all others	⟐

◈ V. Lifestyle Camouflage

Task	Complete?
Wear neutral, quality clothing with no loud logos	◈
Drive a modest car or ride serviceable transportation	◈
Live in a safe but non-showy neighborhood	◈
Keep digital flexing (earnings screenshots, lifestyle posts) to zero	◈
Downplay your profession when asked ("I work in operations/strategy/etc.")	◈
Never discuss your income, investments, or plans in casual conversations	◈

⟐ VI. Security & Contingency

Task	Complete?
Maintain a physical emergency go-bag with backup documents and prepaid cards	⟐
Keep a digital legacy plan with access instructions for your trusted executor	⟐
Store copies of ID, passwords, business plans, and contracts offline	⟐
Maintain 3–6 months of living expenses in a separate, silent "extraction account"	⟐
Rotate passwords and test digital backups at least quarterly	⟐
Schedule a monthly audit of your stealth systems and public exposure	⟐

⟐ VII. Communication Tactics

Task	Complete?
Speak about wealth-building in generalities, not specifics	⟐
Never announce plans until after they're complete	⟐
Maintain silence in the face of probing financial questions	⟐
Create a "default answer" for what you do that reveals nothing	⟐
Use written SOPs (standard operating procedures) for all key systems	⟐

⟐ VIII. Legal & Legacy Cloaking

Task	Complete?
Have a living trust that owns your major assets	⟐
Use a pour-over will to funnel additional assets into the trust	⟐
Designate a digital executor to handle online accounts after death	⟐
Keep all estate documents updated, signed, and stored in multiple secure locations	⟐
Store all crypto seed phrases in physical form (not digital files)	⟐

⟐ Final Reflection: Stealth Wealth Score
Count the total number of checkboxes marked:

- **40–50 boxes**: ⟐ *You are fully cloaked. No one can trace your wealth, and your empire is silent and bulletproof.*
- **30–39 boxes**: ⟐ *Excellent stealth. You're operating with strategic clarity. Minor vulnerabilities remain.*
- **20–29 boxes**: ⟐ *You're quiet—but still exposed in key areas. It's time to reinforce your systems.*
- **0–19 boxes**: ⟐ *You're loud, vulnerable, and traceable. Start the Silence Protocol now.*

⟐ Final Reminder:

Stealth wealth isn't about being secretive.
It's about being **so secure, so silent, and so structured** that no amount of noise can shake what you've built.

Complete this checklist every 90 days.
Update it as your empire grows.
Let no one track your ascent—until the only evidence of your power...
is the **results they can't explain.**

Appendix B – MiB-Inspired Passive Income Ideas

From Digital Galaxies to Earth-Bound Assets

In the *Men in Black* universe, agents don't clock in and out. They operate in the background—efficient, autonomous, and funded by systems that never sleep. Their power doesn't depend on presence. It's embedded in infrastructure. It's encoded into operations.

And that's exactly how your income should function.

This appendix provides a classified collection of **MiB-inspired passive income ideas**, built around one mission: **to make money quietly, consistently, and without dependency on your time or physical presence**.

Whether you're navigating digital galaxies or planting roots in real-world assets, these streams give you leverage. These are income ideas designed to work while you disappear into silence, travel across timelines, or simply rest in a world that can't track your wealth.

◈ SECTION I: Digital Galaxy Streams

Code it once. Collect forever.

1. Microbook Publishing Under Pseudonyms

Write and publish short books (10–50 pages) on niche topics using platforms like Amazon KDP or Lulu.
Topics: magick, self-help, survival, fandoms, guides, astrology.

- Tools: Scrivener, Atticus, Canva
- Stealth Upgrade: Use multiple pen names to protect branding
- Income Style: Royalties every 30–60 days

◈ *"Galactic briefings disguised as books—earning forever while you vanish."*

2. Print-on-Demand Merchandise

Create designs, quotes, or artwork and upload them to platforms like Redbubble, TeePublic, and Printify.

- Focus: Niche aesthetics (MiB quotes, alien lore, "classified energy" themes)
- Tools: Canva, Midjourney, Creative Fabrica
- Stealth Upgrade: Operate under a silent brand name, not your personal identity

◈ *"Let Earthlings wear your designs while you collect royalties from the shadows."*

3. AI-Generated Audio Libraries

Use AI voice tools to create guided meditations, affirmations, sci-fi soundscapes, or alien communication recordings. Sell on sites like Gumroad, Ko-fi, or as a subscription on Patreon.

- Tools: ElevenLabs, Descript, Soundraw
- Niche Ideas: "Alien Language Sleep Frequencies," "Agent Affirmations"
- Bonus: Bundle audio + PDF to boost perceived value

◈ *"When your voice is coded with calm, they'll pay to hear what no one else can say."*

4. Alien Lore Email Series (Auto-Monetized Newsletter)

Set up an automated newsletter that sends cosmic teachings, MiB-inspired life advice, or financial tactics in "mission brief" format.

- Tools: ConvertKit, Beehiiv
- Monetize through affiliate links, premium subscriptions, or course funnels
- Bonus: Offer "classified files" as digital products

◈ *"Broadcast interdimensional wisdom. Let humans pay to feel initiated."*

5. Encrypted Course Platforms

Create an evergreen video course that teaches something specific, in an ultra-thematic style.

Ideas:

- "How to Disappear Digitally"
- "Stealth Wealth Blueprint for Creators"
- "Alien Business Models: Income Streams That Don't Exist (Yet)"
- Platforms: Thinkific, Teachable, Skool
- Upgrade: Sell access via secret link, under a decoy site

◈ *"Your intelligence becomes their freedom—and your royalties."*

⟐ SECTION II: Earth-Bound Passive Systems

Silent ownership of grounded reality.

6. Land Leasing (Unimproved Property)

Purchase low-cost rural land and lease it for:

- RV camping
- Billboard placement
- Solar or antenna towers
- Tiny home off-grid rentals
- Platforms: LandWatch, Zillow, Raw Land Network
- Bonus: Hold title under an LLC for anonymity

⟐ *"Own Earth's forgotten places. Let others fund their dreams on your soil."*

7. Royalty Rights Acquisition

Buy music, book, or patent royalties from creators or resellers.

- Platforms: Royalty Exchange, SongVest, eBay (for low-tier rights)
- Focus: Children's books, niche sound effects, old domain bundles

⟐ *"Invisible contracts that pay you forever. No stage, no spotlight."*

8. Vending Machine Networks

Own and operate vending machines in small clusters at local businesses, laundromats, schools, or apartment buildings.

- Upgrade: Use healthy snacks, themed designs (MiB-branded = unforgettable)
- Outsource restocking or use digital payment-only machines

⟐ *"Machines working while you're off-grid. No employee drama, just earnings."*

9. Silent Airbnb Co-Hosting or Subleasing

Rent or manage properties for others without owning them. You handle bookings, systems, and communication behind the scenes.

- Platforms: Airbnb, Guesty
- Stealth Upgrade: White-label the service under a private brand

⟐ *"Let others host. You manage the matrix."*

10. ATM Route Ownership

Buy and install ATMs at small venues. Earn passive fees per transaction.

- Requires: $2–5K per machine, contracts with local businesses
- Upgrade: Add crypto ATM features for the niche crowd
- Bonus: Maintain via 3rd party service to stay invisible

⟐ *"Every swipe funds your next move—and no one knows who placed the machine."*

◈ SECTION III: Hybrid & Experimental Streams

Between galaxies and ground—creative models for the new age.

11. Galactic Themed Subscription Boxes

Create and ship monthly boxes of curated items: "Agent Survival Kits," "Alien Snacks," "Conspiracy Gear," or "MiB Mindset Manuals."

- Platforms: Cratejoy, Subbly
- Niche Tactic: Include exclusive items not found anywhere else (e.g. fake clearance badges, briefing folders, "top secret" files)

◈ *"Sell mystery. Send mission packs. Control curiosity—and monetize it."*

12. Licensing Sci-Fi Art or Worlds

Build your own fictional universe. License out your lore, characters, or visuals to game developers, authors, or merch stores.

- Platforms: ArtStation, CreativeMarket, StoryMarket
- Tools: Midjourney, Artbreeder, LoreForge
- Bonus: Offer commercial use rights at tiered levels

◈ *"Your mind becomes mythology. Others build with it—and pay to do so."*

13. Buy-and-Disappear eCommerce (No Face Needed)

Set up a faceless Shopify or Etsy store selling digital or drop-shipped MiB-style products—posters, encrypted journals, cosmic planners, tactical bags.

- Tools: Zendrop, Canva, Printful
- Tactic: Bundle products into "classified collections"
- Stealth: Customer never sees your face or personal brand

◈ *"You don't run a shop. You run an operation. And it pays... quietly."*

◈ Final Mission Debrief: How to Choose Your Streams
Use this 5-point MiB Metric to evaluate each opportunity:

Metric	Questions to Ask	Ideal Rating
Visibility	Can I do this without revealing my identity or face?	Low
Automation	Can I set it and let it run without daily work?	High
Scalability	Can it grow without requiring more of *me*?	High
Diversification	Does it complement other streams or protect against collapse?	High
Resilience	Would it survive if I disappeared for 30 days?	Yes

If the income source hits 4 or more of these metrics—you've found a viable MiB-level passive stream.

◈ **Final Directive:**

You don't have to be seen to be paid.
You don't have to go viral to go sovereign.
You don't have to chase. You **build systems that attract.**

When you install passive income that runs silently, endlessly, and without ego...
You become **exactly what they fear most:**

A ghost who thrives.
A shadow who profits.
An agent of abundance—moving undetected.

Briefcase loaded.
Streams deployed.
Mission income: initiated.

Message from the Author:

I hope you enjoyed this book, I love astrology and knew there was not a book such as this out on the shelf. I love metaphysical items as well. Please check out my other books:

-Life of Government Benefits

-My life of Hell

-My life with Hydrocephalus

-Red Sky

-World Domination:Woman's rule

-World Domination:Woman's Rule 2: The War

-Life and Banishment of Apophis: book 1

-The Kidney Friendly Diet

-The Ultimate Hemp Cookbook

-Creating a Dispensary(legally)

-Cleanliness throughout life: the importance of showering from childhood to adulthood.

-Strong Roots: The Risks of Overcoddling children

-Hemp Horoscopes: Cosmic Insights and Earthly Healing

- Celestial Hemp Navigating the Zodiac: Through the Green Cosmos

-Astrological Hemp: Aligning The Stars with Earth's Ancient Herb

-The Astrological Guide to Hemp: Stars, Signs, and Sacred Leaves

-Green Growth: Innovative Marketing Strategies for your Hemp Products and Dispensary

-Cosmic Cannabis

-Astrological Munchies

-Henry The Hemp

-Zodiacal Roots: The Astrological Soul Of Hemp

- **Green Constellations: Intersection of Hemp and Zodiac**

-Hemp in The Houses: An astrological Adventure Through The Cannabis Galaxy

-Galactic Ganja Guide

Heavenly Hemp
Zodiac Leaves
Doctor Who Astrology
Cannastrology
Stellar Satvias and Cosmic Indicas
Celestial Cannabis: A Zodiac Journey
AstroHerbology: The Sky and The Soil: Volume 1
AstroHerbology:Celestial Cannabis:Volume 2
Cosmic Cannabis Cultivation
The Starry Guide to Herbal Harmony: Volume 1
The Starry Guide to Herbal Harmony: Cannabis Universe: Volume 2
Yugioh Astrology: Astrological Guide to Deck, Duels and more
Nightmare Mansion: Echoes of The Abyss
Nightmare Mansion 2: Legacy of Shadows
Nightmare Mansion 3: Shadows of the Forgotten
Nightmare Mansion 4: Echoes of the Damned
The Life and Banishment of Apophis: Book 2
Nightmare Mansion: Halls of Despair
Healing with Herb: Cannabis and Hydrocephalus
Planetary Pot: Aligning with Astrological Herbs: Volume 1
Fast Track to Freedom: 30 Days to Financial Independence Using AI, Assets, and Agile Hustles
Cosmic Hemp Pathways
How to Become Financially Free in 30 Days: 10,000 Paths to Prosperity
Zodiacal Herbage: Astrological Insights: Volume 1
Nightmare Mansion: Whispers in the Walls
The Daleks Invade Atlantis
Henry the hemp and Hydrocephalus

10X The Kidney Friendly Diet
Cannabis Universe: Adult coloring book

Hemp Astrology: The Healing Power of the Stars

Zodiacal Herbage: Astrological Insights: Cannabis Universe: Volume 2

Planetary Pot: Aligning with Astrological Herbs: Cannabis Universes: Volume 2

Doctor Who: Convergence Protocol – The Replicator War

Nightmare Mansion: Curse of the Blood Moon

The Celestial Stoner: A Guide to the Zodiac

Cosmic Pleasures: Sex Toy Astrology for Every Sign

Hydrocephalus Astrology: Navigating the Stars and Healing Waters

Lapis and the Mischievous Chocolate Bar

Celestial Positions: Sexual Astrology for Every Sign

Apophis's Shadow Work Journal: : A Journey of Self-Discovery and Healing

Kinky Cosmos: Sexual Kink Astrology for Every Sign

Digital Cosmos: The Astrological Digimon Compendium

Stellar Seeds: The Cosmic Guide to Growing with Astrology

Apophis's Daily Gratitude Journal

Cat Astrology: Feline Mysteries of the Cosmos

The Cosmic Kama Sutra: An Astrological Guide to Sexual Positions

Unleash Your Potential: A Guided Journal Powered by AI Insights

Whispers of the Enchanted Grove

Cosmic Pleasures: An Astrological Guide to Sexual Kinks

369, 12 Manifestation Journal

Whisper of the nocturne journal(blank journal for writing or drawing)

The Boogey Book

Locked In Reflection: A Chastity Journey Through Locktober

Generating Wealth Quickly:How to Generate $100,000 in 24 Hours

Star Magic: Harness the Power of the Universe

The Flatulence Chronicles: A Fart Journal for Self-Discovery

The Doctor and The Death Moth

Seize the Day: A Personal Seizure Tracking Journal

The Ultimate Boogeyman Safari: A Journey into the Boogie World and Beyond

Whispers of Samhain: 1,000 Spells of Love, Luck, and Lunar Magic: Samhain Spell Book

Apophis's guides:Witch's Spellbook Crafting Guide for Halloween

Frost & Flame: The Enchanted Yule Grimoire of 1000 Winter Spells

The Ultimate Boogey Goo Guide & Spooky Activities for Halloween Fun

Harmony of the Scales: A Libra's Spellcraft for Balance and Beauty

The Enchanted Advent: 36 Days of Christmas Wonders

Nightmare Mansion: The Labyrinth of Screams

Harvest of Enchantment: 1,000 Spells of Gratitude, Love, and Fortune for Thanksgiving

The Boogey Chronicles: A Journal of Nightly Encounters and Shadowy Secrets

The 12 Days of Financial Freedom: A Step-by-Step Christmas Countdown to Transform Your Finances

Sigil of the Eternal Spiral Blank Journal

A Christmas Feast: Timeless Recipes for Every Meal

Holiday Stress-Free Solutions: A Survival Guide to Thriving During the Festive Season

Yu-Gi-Oh! Holiday Gifting Mastery: The Ultimate Guide for Fans and Newcomers Alike

Holiday Harmony: A Hydrocephalus Survival Guide for the Festive Season

Celestial Craft: The Witch's Almanac for 2025 – A Cosmic Guide to Manifestations, Moons, and Mystical Events

Doctor Who: The Toymaker's Winter Wonderland

Tulsa King Unveiled: A Thrilling Guide to Stallone's Mafia Masterpiece

Pendulum Craft: A Complete Guide to Crafting and Using Personalized Divination Tools

Nightmare Mansion: Santa's Eternal Eve

Starlight Noel: A Cosmic Journey through Christmas Mysteries

The Dark Architect: Unlocking the Blueprint of Existence

Surviving the Embrace: The Ultimate Guide to Encounters with The Hugging Molly

The Enchanted Codex: Secrets of the Craft for Witches, Wiccans, and Pagans

Harvest of Gratitude: A Complete Thanksgiving Guide

Yuletide Essentials: A Complete Guide to an Authentic and Magical Christmas

Celestial Smokes: A Cosmic Guide to Cigars and Astrology

Living in Balance: A Comprehensive Survival Guide to Thriving with Diabetes Insipidus

Cosmic Symbiosis: The Venom Zodiac Chronicles

The Cursed Paw of Ambition

Cosmic Symbiosis: The Astrological Venom Journal

Celestial Wonders Unfold: A Stargazer's Guide to the Cosmos (2024-2029)

The Ultimate Black Friday Prepper's Guide: Mastering Shopping Strategies and Savings

Cosmic Sales: The Astrological Guide to Black Friday Shopping

Legends of the Corn Mother and Other Harvest Myths

Whispers of the Harvest: The Corn Mother's Journal

The Evergreen Spellbook

The Doctor Meets the Boogeyman

The White Witch of Rose Hall's SpellBook

The Gingerbread Golem's Shadow: A Study in Sweet Darkness

The Gingerbread Golem Codex: An Academic Exploration of Sweet Myths

The Gingerbread Golem Grimoire: Sweet Magicks and Spells for the Festive Witch

The Curse of the Gingerbread Golem

10-minute Christmas Crafts for kids

Christmas Crisis Solutions: The Ultimate Last-Minute Survival Guide

Gingerbread Golem Recipes: Holiday Treats with a Magical Twist

The Infinite Key: Unlocking Mystical Secrets of the Ages

Enchanted Yule: A Wiccan and Pagan Guide to a Magical and Memorable Season

Dinosaurs of Power: Unlocking Ancient Magick

Astro-Dinos: The Cosmic Guide to Prehistoric Wisdom

Gallifrey's Yule Logs: A Festive Doctor Who Cookbook

The Dino Grimoire: Secrets of Prehistoric Magick

The Gift They Never Knew They Needed

The Gingerbread Golem's Culinary Alchemy: Enchanting Recipes for a Sweetly Dark Feast

A Time Lord Christmas: Holiday Adventures with the Doctor

Krampusproofing Your Home: Defensive Strategies for Yule

Silent Frights: A Collection of Christmas Creepypastas to Chill Your Bones

Santa Raptor's Jolly Carnage: A Dino-Claus Christmas Tale

Prehistoric Palettes: A Dino Wicca Coloring Journey

The Christmas Wishkeeper Chronicles

The Starlight Sleigh: A Holiday Journey

Elf Secrets: The True Magic of the North Pole

Candy Cane Conjurations

Cooking with Kids: Recipes Under 20 Minutes

Doctor Who: The TARDIS Confiscation

The Anxiety First Aid Kit: Quick Tools to Calm Your Mind

Frosty Whispers: A Winter's Tale

The Infinite Key: Unlocking the Secrets to Prosperity, Resilience, and Purpose

The Grasping Void: Why You'll Regret This Purchase

Astrology for Busy Bees: Star Signs Simplified

The Instant Focus Formula: Cut Through the Noise

The Secret Language of Colors: Unlocking the Emotional Codes

Sacred Fossil Chronicles: Blank Journal

The Christmas Cottage Miracle

Feeding Frenzy: Graboid-Inspired Recipes

Manifest in Minutes: The Quick Law of Attraction Guide

The Symbiote Chronicles: Doctor Who's Venomous Journey

Think Tiny, Grow Big: The Minimalist Mindset

The Energy Key: Unlocking Limitless Motivation

New Year, New Magic: Manifesting Your Best Year Yet

Unstoppable You: Mastering Confidence in Minutes

Infinite Energy: The Secret to Never Feeling Drained

Lightning Focus: Mastering the Art of Productivity in a Distracted World

Saturnalia Manifestation Magick: A Guide to Unlocking Abundance During the Solstice

Graboids and Garland: The Ultimate Tremors-Themed Christmas Guide

12 Nights of Holiday Magic

The Power of Pause: 60-Second Mindfulness Practices

The Quick Reset: How to Reclaim Your Life After Burnout

The Shadow Eater: A Tale of Despair and Survival

The Micro-Mastery Method: Transform Your Skills in Just Minutes a Day

Reclaiming Time: How to Live More by Doing Less

Chronovore: The Eternal Nexus

The Mind Reset: Unlocking Your Inner Peace in a Chaotic World
Confidence Code: Building Unshakable Self-Belief
Baby the Vampire Terrier
Baby the Vampire Terrier's Christmas Adventure
Celestial Streams: The Content Creator's Astrology Manual
The Wealth Whisperer: Unlocking Abundance with Everyday Actions
The Energy Equation: Maximize Your Output Without Burning Out
The Happiness Algorithm: Science-Backed Steps to Joyful Living
Stress-Free Success: Achieving Goals Without Anxiety
Mindful Wealth: The New Blueprint for Financial Freedom
The Festive Flavors of New Year: A Culinary Celebration
The Master's Gambit: Keys of Eternal Power
Shadowed Secrets: Groundhog Day Mysteries
Beneath the Burrow: Lessons from the Groundhog
Spring's Whispers: The Groundhog's Prediction
The Limitless Mindset: Unlock Your Untapped Potential
The Focus Funnel: How to Cut Through Chaos and Get Results
Bold Moves: Building Courage to Live on Your Terms
The Daily Shift: Simple Practices for Lasting Transformation
The Quarter-Life Reset: Thriving in Your 20s and 30s
The Art of Shadowplay: Building Your Own Personal Myth
The Eternal Loop: Finding Purpose in Repetition
Burrowing Wisdom: Life Lessons from the Groundhog
Shadow Work: A Groundhog Day Perspective
Love in Bloom: 5-Minute Romantic Gestures
The Shadowspell Codex: Secrets of Forbidden Magick
The Burnout Cure: Finding Balance in a Busy World
The Groundhog Prophecy: Unlocking Seasonal Secrets
Nog Tales: The Spirited History of Eggnog
Six More Weeks: Embracing Seasonal Transitions
The Lumivian Chronicles: Fragments of the Fifth Dimension

Money on Your Mind: A Beginner's Guide to Wealth
The Focus Fix: Breaking Through Distraction
January's Spirit Keepers: Mystical Protectors of the Cold
Creativity Unchained: Unlocking Your Wildest Ideas in 2025
Manifestation Mastery: 365 Days to Rewrite Your Reality
The Groundhog's Mirror: Reflecting on Change
The Weeping Angels' Christmas Curse
Burrowed in Time: A Groundhog Day Journey
Heartbeats: Poems to Share with Your Valentine
Dino Wicca: The Sacred Grimoire of Prehistoric Magick
Courage of the Pride: Finding Your Inner Roar
The Lion's Leap: Bold Moves for Big Results
Healthy Hustle: Achieving Without Overworking
Practical Manifesting: Turning Dreams into Reality in 2025
Jurassic Pharaohs: Unlocking the Magick of Ancient Egypt and Dino Wicca
The Happiness Equation: Small Changes for Big Joy
The Confidence Compass: Finding Your Inner Strength
Whispers in the Hollow: Tales of the Forgotten Beasts
Echoes from the Hollow: The Return of Forgotten Beasts
The Hollow Ascendant: The Rise of the Forgotten Beasts
The Relationship Reset: Building Better Connections
Mastering the Morning: How to Win the Day Before 8 AM
The Shadow's Dance: Groundhog Day Symbolism
Cupid's Kitchen: Quick Valentine's Day Recipes
Valentine's Day on a Budget: Love Without Breaking the Bank
Astrocraft: Aligning the Stars in the World of Minecraft
Forecasting Life: Groundhog Day Reflections
Bleeding Hearts: Twisted Tales of Valentine's Terror
Herbal Smoke Revolution: The Ultimate Guide to Nature's Cigarette Alternative
Winter's Wrath: The Complete Survival Blueprint for Extreme Freezes.

The Groundhog's Shadow: A Tale of Seasons
Burrowed Insights: Wisdom from the Groundhog
Sensual Strings: The Art of Erotic Bondage
Whispered Flames: Unlocking the Power of Fire Play
Forgotten Shadows: A Guide to Cryptids Lost to Time
Six Weeks of Secrets: Groundhog Day's Hidden Messages
Shadows and Cycles: Groundhog Day Reflections
The Art of Love Letters: Crafting the Perfect Message
Romantic Getaways at Home: Turning Your Space into Paradise
Purrfect Brews: A Cat Lover's Guide to Coffee and Companionship
The Groundhog's Wisdom: Timeless Lessons for Modern Life
The Shadow Oracle: Groundhog Day as a Predictor
Emerging from the Burrow: A Journey of Renewal
The Language of Love: Learning Your Partner's Love Style
Authorpreneur: The Ultimate Blueprint for Writing, Publishing, and Thriving as an Author
Weathering the Seasons: Groundhog Day Perspectives
Valentine's Day Magic: A Guide to Romantic Rituals
The Shadow Chronicles: Stories of Groundhog Day
Love and Laughter: Fun Games for Valentine's Day
AstroRealty: Unlocking the Stars for Property Success
The Groundhog's Path: A Guide to Seasonal Balance
Groundhog Day Diaries: Reflections in the Shadow
The Groundhog's Light: Illuminating the Path Ahead
Valentine's Traditions from Around the World
AI Wealth Revolution: Unlocking the Trillionaire Mindset
Love Rekindled: Reigniting Passion in Relationships
Single and Thriving: Self-Love on Valentine's Day
Emerald Legends: Mystical Tales of Ireland
Green Alchemy: Harnessing Nature's Magic
The Hearts of Horror: A Valentine's Day Nightmare

The Leprechaun's Guide to Wealth and Wisdom
Dancing with the Sidhe: Celebrating the Otherworld
Shamrocks and Shadows: Mysteries of the Green Isle
Emerald Energy: Harnessing Luck and Growth
The Gingerbread Golem's Valentine: A Sweetheart's Guide to Love and Enchantment
The Celtic Knot: Weaving Life and Destiny
Green Fire: Elemental Magic for St. Patrick's Day
Clover Chronicles: Finding Your Inner Luck
Ireland's Mystical Creatures: A Field Guide
Gingerbread Golem's Love Almanac
Prowl and Thrive: The Lion's Guide to Success
Love Alchemy: Transforming Your Life Through Heart Energy
WORLD DOMINATION: Woman's Rule 3:The New Life
The Midnight Rose: A Guide to Lunar Love Spells
The Forbidden Letters: Writing Your Own Love Prophecy
Luck and Lore: St. Patrick's Day for Modern Mystics
The Green Path: A Pagan Celebration of Renewal
The Dark Architect's Guide to Reprogramming Reality
Prankster's Paradise: A Guide to Harmless Hijinks
Manifest Your Reality: The Law of Attraction Simplified
The TARDIS Owner's Manual: Understanding the Doctor's Ship: *A complete guide to the TARDIS, its technology, secrets, and mysteries*
Starlit Romance: Astrology Secrets for Finding True Love
The Time Lord's Atlas: A Complete Guide to the Whoniverse: ***A breakdown of the locations, planets, and dimensions explored in Doctor Who***
Sweetheart Shadows: The Dark Side of Love and Attraction
February Fire: Reigniting Passion in Every Area of Life
The Self-Love Toolkit: 5 Ways to Embrace Who You Are
February Sparks: Ignite Your Dreams in 28 Days

March to Success: A 31-Day Action Blueprint
Ancient Paths: The 13 Sacred Principles of Dino Wicca
Echoes of Tomorrow: Navigating the AI Revolution
The Wellness Blueprint: Balancing Mind, Body, and Soul
Green Horizons: Sustainable Living for a Better Tomorrow
The AI Wealth Code: How to Make Millions with Automation
AI-Powered Creativity: Writing, Art, and Music for Profit
Extinction Rites: Rebirthing Your Soul Through Prehistoric Magick
Sacred Serpents tarot
Celestial Enchantment blank journal
Star Strains
Culinary Journeys: Exploring Global Flavors at Home
The Hollowvale Curse
The Hollowvale Harvest
The Egg of Transformation: Awakening Your Inner Power
Blooming Into Power: A Wiccan Guide to Spring Awakening
The Nightmare Nexus: The Third Doctor's Perilous Haunting
Digital Detox: Reclaiming Your Life in a Connected World
Ostara's Path: Walking the Spiral of Renewal
The Sacred Hare
Financial Freedom: Building Wealth in the Modern Age
Spring's Cauldron: Stirring the Waters of Change
The Hollowvale Pact
Quantum Consciousness: The Science of Reality Shifting
The Hollowvale Hunger
The Sacred Waters Within: A Witch's Guide to Hydrocephalus Magick
The Raven's Nest: Building a Life of Unshakable Stability
AI and the Human Mind: The Future of Intelligence
The Hollowvale Reckoning
Timeless Love: Building and Maintaining Lasting Relationships

The Raven's Roar: Unlocking Unstoppable Confidence
Raven Sight: Awakening Intuition and Inner Wisdom
The Butterfly Effect: Small Changes, Big Transformations
Taming the Boogeyman: How to Conquer Your Inner Fears
The Magick of Green: Awakening Earth's Energy in You
The Entrepreneurial Mindset: Secrets to Business Success
The Hollowvale End
The Shadow Luck Ritual: Reclaiming Power from Your Dark Side
Spring Magick for Beginners: A Simple Guide to Seasonal Energy Work
Doctor Who: The Hollowvale Conundrum
The March of Miracles: Unlocking Synchronicities in Spring
Unveiling the Cosmos: A Guide to Stargazing and Space Exploration
The Ultimate Guide to Surviving an Economic Collapse
The AI Gold Rush: How to Profit from the AI Revolution
Bastet's Shadow: The Hidden Power of Feline Magick
The Bastet Codex: Unlocking the Goddess's Magickal Secrets
Purring Spells: Harnessing Bastet's Healing Frequencies
Bastet's Nine Lives: Rebirth, Transformation, and Immortality Spells
Primal Currents: Hydrocephalus Magick in the Path of Dino Wicca
The Digital Gold Rush: Mastering E-Commerce and Online Sales
Future Shock: Adapting to the Next Decade of Change
The Quantum Mindset: Think Like a Billionaire
Sacred Motherhood: Awakening the Divine Feminine Within
The Mother's Spellbook: Enchantments for Love, Protection, and Prosperity
The Witch's Guide to Parenting: Raising Empowered and Intuitive Children

The Magick of Motherhood: Reclaiming Your Power Through Rituals
The Pagan Path to Self-Love: A Goddess's Guide to Worth and Confidence
Wild Woman Magick: Unleashing Your Primal Power
The Money Magnet Blueprint: Unlocking Unlimited Wealth
Biohacking 101: Unlock Your Body's Full Potential
The Wild Father: A Pagan Guide to Strength and Wisdom
The Sacred Masculine: Unlocking Your Inner Power
The Druid's Compass
The Warrior's Mindset
The Father's Fire
Odin's Path
Ancestral Bonds
The House That Whispers
The Magician's Code
The Wild Hunt
The Green Man's Path
The Altar of Success
The Shadow and the Sword
The High Priestess's Guide to Energy Healing
The Lunar Mother
The Sacred Self-Care Grimoire
The Womb Wisdom Codex
The Wheel of the Mother
The Witch's Guide to Manifestation
The Q2 Reset
The Ultimate Guide to AI-Powered Passive Income
Escape the 9-5
AI Feline Fortunes
The Tear-Stained Grimoire
Razorblade Runes
Cemetery Sirens

The Midnight Wristwatch
The Town That Forgets
AI Horror & Creepypasta
The Hollow Frequency
The Breach Echo
The Quiet Between Worlds
The Sigil of Tharan-Khul
Summon the Vault of Y'ha'ten
The Becoming Codex
The Profit of Az'ra-nar
The Drowned Logos
Echoes of the Eldritch Will
The Deep Ledger
Necronomicon of Networth
Covenant of the Wealthwyrm
The Whisperer's Manifesto
The Rites of Azh-K'luth
The Ark of the Crawling Coin
The Tithe of Shadows
Inkheart Abyss
The Timewinds of Y'ha-nthlei
The Spiral Labyrinth of Azag-Nirrh
The Gallifreyan Heresy of the Black Pharaoh
The Psalms of Nyog-Sotha
Black Rain Alchemy
The Infinite Maw
The Entropic Blueprint
The Oracle of Sh'guul
The Book of Breach
The Drowned Saint's Testament
Dreamcraft of the Sleeper God
The Silence Market
Cthonomics: The Dark Wealth Algorithm

Invocation of the Ten-Eyed King
Wealthbound to the Wyrm Below
Become the Unnameable
Codex of the Sovereign Flame
Rituals of Relentless Becoming
The Shadow Ascends
The Eyes Beneath You
The Will That Wakes Worlds
Silence Is a Weapon
The Mirror That Screams
The Whisper Between Moments
The Mind That Devours Fear
The Myth of the Finished Self
The Architect of Your Madness
The Voice You've Buried
The Discipline of Madness
Stormborn: Awakening Your Inner Tempest
The Mind That Ate Time
Unbind Your Becoming
The Pact You Owe Yourself
The Devourer's Diet
The Acid That Carves the Path
The Tower You Must Burn
The Breath Between Worlds
Speak Like the Deep
The Labyrinth Within
The Spine of the Sea God
Rejection Is a Portal
The Crown You Refused
The Scar Is the Spell
The Lightless Flame
The Habit of Becoming Horrific
ChickenJockey Chaos

The Gatekeeper Within
You Are Not Your Name
The Compass of the Mad
The Archive of Unsent Letters
What the Mirror Can't Show You
The Knife You Needed
Worship Nothing, Become Everything
The Other Voice
The Body the World Forgot
The Vein of the Void
The Black Bone Codex
The Puzzle of the Hidden Self (Millennium Puzzle)
The Eye That Sees the Lie *(Millennium Eye)*
The Ring of Return (Millennium Ring)
The Rod of Relentless Will *(Millennium Rod)*
The Tally of the Soul (Millennium Tauk/Necklace)
The Key to the Locked Timeline (Millennium Key)
The Scale of Sacred Decisions (Millennium Scales)
Inferno Bites: The UnOfficial Minecraft Lava Cookbook
Rot in the Attic
Prana: The Hidden Force of Your Infinite Self
The Shadow Realm Within: Transforming Darkness Into Destiny
The Borderland Collapse
Claws of Protection: Bastet's Defensive Magick
Mr. Ring-a-Ding's Madness
Yugioh Astrology: Celestial Deckcraft and Duel Destiny (2026–2027 Edition)
The Seal You Signed: Unlocking the Power You Once Feared
The Puzzle of Infinite Minds: Unlocking the Mentalism Hidden Within
The Eye That Mirrors the All: Secrets of Inner Reflection
Doctor Who: The Toymaker's Broadcast

Rootwake: The Carbon Covenant
Skitter Logic: Unlearning the Fear That Built You
Doctor Who: The World That Froths
Rootwake: The Fizz That Rewrites Flesh
Rootwake: Frothfather of the World
The Holly Pact: Blood Beneath the Mistletoe
The 2nd Mass Principle: Building Unbreakable Tribes
Web of Wits: A Survival Guide to Encounters with Anasi the Spider (Aunt Nancy)
The Hexbreaking Handbook: Effective Spells to Remove Curses
Pop Alchemy: Transform Your Life One Sip at a Time
The Mason Code: Leading in Unleadable Times
Petosiris and the Fifth Chamber of Thoth
The Ether Seed Within
The Parent of Tomorrow
Petosiris's Pyramid of Perpetual Wealth
Unlearn the World
Grimoire of the Hollow Tongue
Zodiac Weeds: Finding Your Strain Through the Stars
Aquarius Rises in the Bank
The Sugar God's Smile
The Skinclock Reversal: Biohacking the Face of Time
Debtburn: How to Obliterate What You Owe Forever
The Ice Cream Oracle: What Your Cone Says About Your Future
Silence Is Sovereignty: The Power of Being Unreadable
The Wind That Whispers Through Stone
Path of the Four Directions
Doctor Who: The Maestro's Symphony of Endings
Oxygen Grail: Breathing to Undo the Clock
Zodiacal Collapse: When Stars Devour Time
Teachings from the Red Sand Silence

Doctor Who: Omega – The Broken Equation
Memory Wipe Your Past: Start Over Like a MiB
Mitochondria Prime: Ignite the Core of Youth
A Nest of Roaches
Grub from the Galaxy: MiB Recipes You'll Never Forget
Whiskers of Power: Bastet's Guide to Inner Sovereignty
The Gift Must Cost Them: Negotiation Through Unequal Exchange
The Worm Guys' Wealth Code: Hustle Like an Alien
Bug Out: The Edgar Method for Ruthless Goal Setting
Weaving Life with Spiderwoman's Pattern
Doctor Who: The Rani's Renaissance
How to Get a Job (If You're a Puppygirl)
Speak Through Others: The Art of Proxy Power
T-Rex Your Trauma: Reclaim the Power of Your Primal Self

Get Some Tarot cards: https://www.makeplayingcards.com/sell/apophis-occult-shop

Get some shirts: https://www.bonfire.com/store/apophis-shirt-emporium/

<u>Instagrams:</u>
@apophis_enterprises,
@apophisbookemporium,
@apophisscardshop
Twitter: @apophisenterpr1
Tiktok:@apophisenterprise
Youtube: @sg1fan23477
Hive: @sg1fan23477
CheeLee: @SG1fan23477

Podcast: Apophis Chat Zone: https://open.spotify.com/show/5zXbrCLEV2xzCp8ybrfHsk?si=fb4d4fdbdce44dec

Newsletter: https://apophiss-newsletter-27c897.beehiiv.com/

If you want to support me or see posts of other projects that I have come over to: **buymeacoffee.com/mpetchinskg**

I post there daily several times a day

Get your Dinowicca or Christmas themed digital products, especially Santa Raptor songs and other musics. Here: **https://sg1fan23477.gumroad.com**

Apophis Yuletide Digital has not only digital Christmas items, but it will have all things with Dinowicca as well as other Digital products.

www.ingramcontent.com/pod-product-compliance
Lightning Source LLC
LaVergne TN
LVHW022225200926
848481LV00006B/2132
9798349462054